T0256388

Career Counseling
Over the Internet

*An Emerging Model for Trusting
and Responding to Online Clients*

Career Counseling
Over the Internet

An Emerging Model for Trusting
and Responding to Online Clients

Patricia Mulcahy Boer

Routledge
Taylor & Francis Group
New York   London

First published by

Lawrence Erlbaum Associates, Inc., Publishers
10 Industrial Avenue
Mahwah, NJ 07430

This edition published 2012 by Routledge

Routledge
Taylor & Francis Group
711 Third Avenue
New York, NY 10017

Routledge
Taylor & Francis Group
27 Church Road, Hove
East Sussex BN3 2FA

Cover design by Kathryn Houghtaling Lacey

Library of Congress Cataloging-in-Publication Data

Boer, Patricia Mulcahy.
Career counseling over the Internet : an emerging model
    for trusting and responding to online clients / Patricia
    Mulcahy Boer.
        p.   cm.
Includes bibliographical references and index.
ISBN 0-8058-3744-2 (cloth. : alk. paper)
ISBN 0-8058-3745-0 (pbk. : alk. paper)
1. Vocational guidance—Computer network resources
    2. Career development—Computer network
    resources. 3. Internet (Computer network)   I. Title.
HF5382.7 .B655   2001
331.7'02'02854678—dc21
                                            00-034767
                                                 CIP

Contents

Part III   Preparing for a Paradigm Shift

Introduction

"When you are moving toward an objective," said Petrus, "it is very important to pay attention to the road. It is the road that teaches us the best way to get there, and the road enriches us as we walk its length .... And it is the same thing when you have an objective in your life. It will turn out to be better or worse depending on the route you choose to reach it and the way you negotiate that route. That's why the second RAM practice is so important; it extracts from what we are used to seeing everyday the secrets that because of our routine, we never see."

—Coelho (1995, p. 36)

In Coelho's international bestseller, *The Pilgrimage, A Contemporary Quest for Ancient Wisdom*, Petrus is the mysterious guide and mentor to Paulo, the book's hero. Together, in Spain, they walk the legendary road to Santiago. Drawing on 11 exercises from the ancient Order of the RAM ® for rigor, A for adoration, and M for mercy), Paulo learns to let the road teach him, thereby discovering self-mastery and what to do with it.

Like Paulo, my experiences as an online career counselor lead me to pay attention to my "road." While walking its twists and turns, I slowed down not wanting "to miss the secrets it might teach me." Reflections about this journey prompt me to share my insights with career counseling professionals, presenting these through interactive research methods. Interactive research methods (reflections in action) in an applied setting (the Internet) offer professionals the best way to examine new practices (*11 lessons from the road*) for the development of theory and practice models on career counseling via the Internet.

Merriam and Simpson (1989) defined interactive research as having several characteristics, which distinguish its methods from other forms of social science research:

1. The researcher serves as a facilitator for problem solving... (and) ... as a catalyst between the research findings and those individuals most likely to benefit or take action from the findings.
2. The results of research are intended for immediate application by those engaged in the research or by those for whom the research was initiated.
3. The design of interactive research is formulated while the research is in progress, rather than being totally predetermined at the outset of the study.

Interactive research methodologies are consistent with still earlier writings by Dewey (1916) who stated: "There is no such thing as genuine knowledge and fruitful understanding except as the offspring of doing ... this is the lesson of the laboratory method, and the lesson which all of education has to learn." To Dewey, the classroom, the boardroom, the gymnasium, the office (the Internet) all are laboratories for learning, places where the learners must be productively involved for learning to occur. Dewey's laboratory methods remain pertinent, particularly, for today's studies on new services emerging via the Internet. These lessons, too, undoubtedly underscore directives from Sussman (1998) that "It is our duty as members of the profession to take an active role in guiding this new method of services delivery."

PURPOSE AND SCOPE

Prompted by Sussman's message and by the lack of research about online career counseling, the purpose of this book is to share my perspective on emerging career counseling practices via the Internet. The book begins by articulating issues in the debate on Internet counseling, giving particular attention to counselor concerns about ethical issues and the client–counselor relationship. Next, it details the 11 necessary competencies and skills for counseling professionals in general, translating these for use online, including the role of assessment, various electronic interventions, and the pros and cons of career counseling via the Web. Specific guidelines are offered for career counselors to implement online. The book concludes with suggestions for continuing research, as well as recommendations for counselor supervision, preparation, and training models as the field makes a paradigm shift. Framed into 10 chapters, 35 question and answer (Q & A) examples are interspersed to bring to life the actual experiences, themes, issues, and questions presented by a global clientele regarding their career development. Each chapter closes with discussion questions for practitioners to consider among themselves or discuss with students in classroom and practice settings.

For many, online career counseling appears a very simple task, similar to answering e-mail messages, something many do everyday as part of their jobs. What is not necessarily apparent is the complexity of knowledge and skill required to respond online, ethically and appropriately everyday, including weekends and holidays. Like Olympic figure skaters gliding across the ice, who make their jumps and turns look easy, the online counselor calls on similar preparation that makes this online art look easy. That preparation is called academic, and professional training coupled with career counseling services for a diverse population of clients. Furthermore, preparation means ongoing continuing education on career theory and counseling skills, research issues, labor market trends, technology resources, knowledge of cultural differences, assessment and reflection on client issues, and consultation for performance improvement. It also means managing the technology, juggling online messages (i.e., prioritizing, analyzing, toggling online for research, cutting/pasting, editing and rereading before responding to clients), as well as tracking/sorting into folders, sometimes rewriting after reflection, and asking for client feedback. My intention is to explain the complexities, challenges, and drawbacks of this medium. My purpose is to add to the emerging body of knowledge on electronic career services, and in particular, Internet career counseling.

OVERVIEW

This book differs from recent career counseling publications in both format and framework. Using a narrative format coupled with interactive research methodologies, practitioner issues are examined in light of the debate on the efficacy of online career counseling services, with my reflections on recent practices formulating the basis for an emerging model. The narrative format was selected to reflect what Paisely (1997) described as the importance of personalizing our history:

The personal component adds the texture we might otherwise ignore. As counseling comes of age as a discipline and as we as counselors acknowledge the diversity of our experience as well as our different ways of knowing, we must also come to a place where we can honor both empirical data and the power of personal narrative. To limit ourselves professionally to one approach also limits our definition of who we are and who we can become. (p. 4)

Personalizing our history is a concept consistent with the notion of influencing public policy advocated by Savickas (1996). In a special publication of *Public Policy and Career Counseling for the Twenty-First Century*, Savickas noted:

Counselors can contribute important perspectives and ideas to the national dialogue about public policy concerning (a) goals for career intervention, (b) who will plan and who will deliver career interventions, and (c) to whom and how career intervention will be made accessible. (p. 4)

To personalize this history and contribute new perspectives, the book is organized into 10 chapters, demonstrating how to integrate and apply 11 career counseling competencies into Internet career counseling services. Three themes further organize the chapters. Part I, Reflections on Practice, offers a philosophical rational for online career counseling. Part II, Translating Reflections Into Practice, defines and demonstrates the practical application of various electronic interventions including attention to online assessment instruments, with comparisons presented between in-person and online counseling skills. Part III, Preparing for a Paradigm Shift, gives attention to research and counselor preparation programs, with examples from clients throughout the book, providing the reader a view of this medium through the eyes of clients.

For instance in Part I, client examples are used to illustrate topics such as the benefits of written text and increased client access with special attention to the online client–counselor relationship. Chapter 1, Articulating Issues in the Debate, identifies the views of leaders, vendors and counselors in the field characterizing the profession at a crossroads. For many, technology is viewed as the catalyst for positive change if "we as members demonstrate new forms of adaptability and creativity in its work" (Watts, 1998).

In chapter 2, Defining the Career Counseling Process, the competencies of career development theory and individual counseling skills set the stage to define specific terms and related concepts. These concepts include the following:

1. The career counseling process
2. Career planning services
3. Measurement and assessment in career counseling
4. WebCounseling
5. Internet career counseling

Q & A examples further illustrate these concepts for practice in a global economy.

Building on chapter 2, chapter 3, Safeguarding the Client–Counselor Relationship, specifies safeguards for this relationship highlighting the importance of following ethical standards, defining boundaries, establishing trust and rapport, and ensuring confidentiality. This chapter also discusses the importance of individual counseling and assessment skills, pointing out the paradox and positive aspects inherent in online services, namely, anonymity. Anonymity allows for unexpected benefits, such as giving clients the freedom to ask core questions and through anonymity the added assurance of confidentiality.

Translating reflections into practice is the organizing theme of the next four chapters. These chapter titles reflect counselor issues and competencies as well as issues posed by online career counseling clients. Competencies include serving diverse populations, coaching/consultation for performance improvement, assessment, and information/resources. For example, chapter 4, Serving International Clients and Diverse Populations, focuses first on understanding and responding to an international clientele. This means attention to immigration issues, not typically addressed in career counseling sessions, such as questions about immigration laws, work permits, visas, recruiters, and companies looking for international candidates. Q & A examples are drawn from an international audience representing pleas for help from India, Russia, Pakistan, China, Mexico, Switzerland, Ghana, Nigeria, Thailand, Sweden, Italy, Austria, and the United Kingdom. The dreams and hopes of these international clients are a reminder that career direction (theirs, ours, and others) begins with a dream for a better life. Individual differences related to gender, sexual orientation, race, ethnicity, and physical and mental capacities are another focus of this chapter, with continuing discussions and examples offered in the following chapters.

Chapter 5, Coaching/Consulting for Performance Improvement, addresses the importance of defining the online skills to serve diverse client populations and issues. This chapter demonstrates how to use these skills, describing a process for helping clients ages 21 to 51 starting out or starting over, with such questions as how to choose a college major, identify internships, graduate schools and/or working with your college/university career centers, as well as initiating an effective job search. "Help! I haven't a clue" was often the first sentence from online clients. Examples of integrating counseling skills with attention to individual differences related to gender, sexual orientation, race, ethnicity, and physical and mental capacities are also included, as well as the role of reflection in practice and need for response on time.

Chapter 6, Understanding the Use of Assessment Online, discusses and clarifies the link between career counseling and testing by defining assessment terms and demonstrating through client examples how online testing is implemented. Chapter 7, Providing Appropriate Information and Referrals, addresses the knowledge and skills considered essential in using technology to assist individuals with career planning. This includes information and referral skills for career planning, job search links, and resources for diverse populations. The chapter also discusses how to research information on education, training, and employment trends; labor market information and resources that provide information about job tasks, functions, salary requirements; and future outlooks.

The third theme of the book, preparing for the paradigm shift, introduces the last three chapters. In these chapters the competencies of supervision, program promotion, management, and implementation are discussed along with the importance of evaluation and research. Starting with chapter 8, Embracing Technology, examples are offered from a sample of 65 messages that were returned due to computer glitches or technology failures, demonstrating one of the barriers or downside of this medium. The chapter also discusses the importance of support for putting a human face on technology in the delivery of career counseling services.

Closely related is chapter 9, Encouraging Qualitative Research, or what professionals can learn from reviewing and reflecting on qualitative studies. An analysis from interactive research methodologies offers suggestions for counselor training, supervision, and the development of practice models.

Chapter 10, Emerging Practice Models, offers a summary of key reflections on 11 lessons from the road with suggestions for practice that reinforces the purpose of the book, valuing online career services as the medium for the 21st century. Throughout the book, samples of client messages and thank you notes demonstrate the helpfulness of the service from the client's perspective. By including reflections on journal notes, this chapter may serve as the beginning of a qualitative study to advance the understanding of this innovative career counseling service. New insights about online services will serve researchers and practitioners alike as we move forward to fulfill the National Career Development Association (NCDA) Mission: "to facilitate the career development of all people across the life span."

AUDIENCES

The book is primarily aimed at career counseling professionals, those practicing in academic and business settings, particularly those interested in the theory and practice of online career services. In academic settings offering graduate classes in career counseling, this volume could serve as a secondary text. With research on Internet services in its infancy, the returned messages noted in chapter 8 as well as the thank you messages highlighted throughout may be of particular interest for academic studies on the benefits and barriers of this technology.

For practitioners, the book offers a handy reference for client questions and/or Internet sites related to frequently asked questions. The book also serves outplacement professionals, particularly those engaged in change management and career self-development. Not having the benefit of career counseling courses or internships, these professionals often find their clients asking the very questions posed by online clients.

The inclusion of Q & A examples may give the book wide appeal to a broad range of other professionals. Also, there may be an audience among the general public interested in self-development and career management. Already, the online format has an audience of 40,000 including students, professionals, and travelers from more than 12 foreign countries.

Acknowledgments

There are several people I want to acknowledge for encouraging my work and, in turn, influencing many observations discussed in this book. I start with my professors at the University of San Diego, who impressed me by the way they lived their values and stressed the importance of giving back to our communities. As living models of their values, they influenced my career decisions and life more than I can say. Also influential were my counseling professors and practicum supervisors, Dr. John C. Jessell, professor of counseling psychology, Indiana State University and Dr. Stanley J. Gross, professor of counseling psychology emeritus and lecturer in counseling psychology at Tufts University. They referred to living one's values, particularly counseling values, as congruence, integration. Their stress was on the importance of trust in the client–counselor relationship. They noted that if we as counselors do not trust our clients, e cannot then expect them to trust us. With this trust in me, I extended trust to my clients, thus experiencing deep satisfaction as I worked with each client at the IUPUI Continuing Education Center for Women and later in private practice. From these clients, too, I owe a tremendous debt about what works to facilitate client growth. And, from my mentors in private practice, the late Harriet Lancaster, MA, AAMFT, and Dr. Royda Crose, counseling psychologist, Ball State University, I learned that counseling is more than a good feeling. It means dealing with one's own issues before attending to those of the client. It means, too, that trusting the process, whether looking at one's issues or trusting clients to examine theirs, takes courage without which there is no insight.

Next, I am indebted to Susan Bryant and Craig Besant, formerly of the Online Career Center and currently with Monster.com. Without their confidence in my practice, what became an unique online career counseling service would not have materialized nor would it be the subject of this book. Nor would the book materialize without enthusiastic responses from online clients. Editors, too, were enthusiastic, particularly Joanetta Hendell, Wordswork Publishing, Indianapolis, and Melinda Adams Merino, Counseling Psychologist Press-Davies Back Publishing, Palo Alto, who referred me to Lawrence Erlbaum Associates (LEA). At LEA, I am indebted most to Senior Editor Anne Duffy who selected my manuscript and made herself available throughout the publication process.

My three daughters, Kathy, Karol, and Virginia were there, too, providing encouragement and support as I pressed forward. Good friends and professional colleagues were also instrumental in the book's progress. Their comments and editorial suggestions were invaluable, particularly those from Peg Darnell, professor of the Technical Writing Program for the School of Engineering, Purdue University. Finally, I am indebted to the online clients I served at OCC.com and currently assist in a coaching role with Monster.com.

Together, all of these special people influence my work and inspire many observations discussed in this study. This publication is dedicated to all of them and in loving memory of my silent partner, my brother, Thomas Joseph Mulcahy, III.

—Patricia M. Boer

PART

I

Reflections on Practice

As a career counseling practitioner and ethnographic researcher, reflections on practice permeate everything I do. For example, when I listen to a client's story, simultaneously I am reflecting on the context of his or her life, individual circumstances, and how these fit with career counseling theories. As I review my notes or texts in a client file I also reflect on their meanings, all the while considering appropriate interventions or resources to help the client move forward. It seems only logical to begin the first chapters of this book with reflection on practice. This organizing theme allows me to share what I have learned as an online career counselor. My rationale for choosing online practice is explained in chapter 1, Articulating the Issues in the Debate. Chapter 2, Career Development Theory, focuses on the first of 11 career counseling competencies expected of a National Certified Career Counselor (NCCC). This chapter emphasizes the appropriateness of online services. providing assurances in chapter 3 about Safeguarding the Client–Counselor Relationship. Actual examples from online practice illustrate and reinforce the importance of online practice to clients. Additional examples are offered in Part II, Translating Reflections into Practice.

1

Articulating Issues in the Debate

There is consensus among counselors that the most satisfying part of our job is being with a client, witnessing the moment when a connection is made. At that moment you see a change in body language, such as posture, facial expression, a sparkle in the eye, all changes signaling the client feels heard and understood. They feel a burden has been lifted. They are freer, ready to focus, and move forward. No outside force, person, or supervisor is necessary to tell you when this happens. You know it. Although it may not happen with every client, when it does, you know clearly that you are doing your job. Theorists identify this moment as building the client–counselor relationship, a relationship built on trust, acceptance, and unconditional positive regard (Crose,1990; Minchin, 1974; Rogers, 1961; Satir, 1972; Tiedeman & Miller-Tiedeman, 1988, 1989). Establishing and building this relationship is not a set of techniques alone. Instead, theorists characterize it as an attitude: Satir called this "nurturance," Crose identified it as "caring," and Minchin, "joining." This special relationship is also characterized by a deep respect for individuals in all their complexities.

FIVE ISSUES MARK THE DEBATE ON INTERNET COUNSELING

Establishing and safeguarding the client-counselor relationship is both the heart of professional life for counselors, and a definition of the client-centered approach to the counseling process (Hansen, Stevic, & Warner, 1976). To counselors, safeguarding the client–counselor relationship is chief among the five core issues in the debate about online counseling, what Bloom (1997) defined as *WebCounseling*. Questions surrounding the client–counselor relationship focus first on how to protect the integrity of the relationship against potential misunderstandings arising from a lack of visual clues and what happens in emergencies when the client is halfway around the globe. Closely related to this issue is the second issue of ethical practice: how to ensure confidentiality and access. Third is technology (both keeping up with its changes and technological failures), as well as billing and termination issues: What impact does technology have on the counseling process? Fourth is research. Because there is virtually no research available, how do we know if WebCounseling is helpful or harmful? Counselor preparation is fifth, including certification to answer how we can make a paradigm shift and/or protect the public interest without legislation.

National Standards

Together, these five issues unleashed an intense debate when the National Board for Certified Counselors (NBCC) approved standards for counseling over the Internet in September 1997. One month later, the Board of Directors of the National Career Development Association (NCDA) approved NCDA *Guidelines for the Use of the Internet For Provision of Career Information and Planning Services*. These guidelines:

1. Outline four major ways to provide career planning services to clients.
2. Differentiate *career planning services* from *career counseling*.
3. List eight multiple means for delivery including:
   - Developer/provider qualifications
   - Access and understanding of environment
   - Content of career counseling and planning services
   - Appropriateness of client for receipt of services via the Internet
   - Appropriate support for the client
   - Clarity of the contract with the client
   - Inclusion of linkages to other websites
   - Use of assessment
4. Add three categories focusing on:
   - Professional and ethical guidelines related to job posting/searching

- Unacceptable counselor behaviors on the internet
- Need for research and review

The debate about online counseling services began long before the development of NBCC and NCDA standards for counseling over the Internet. Approval of new standards simply gave permission for professionals to formally express their concerns. Reaching back a decade earlier, the debate started when vendors of psychological assessments and career interest inventories began marketing online capabilities. Companies like Consulting Psychology Press, now Consulting Psychology Press-Davies Black Publishing (CPP-DB) and the National Scoring Center (NSC) were among the first to target online assessment instruments to college and university counseling and career centers. Online administration and scoring options offered increased access to users. For test administrators and counselors, the service offered a confidential and expedient method to retrieve and review assessment results with clients. Online assessments thereby served as tools for counselors rather than a replacement for their services. Yet not all counselors welcomed this direction.

The Growth of Electronic Interventions

In the years since, online career counseling services evolved and flourished, quickly becoming part of the career guidance movement in the United States. Today, an array of electronic career interventions, or online services, is available to the public. Although many, these interventions are not the focus of this chapter, nor specifically germane to key issues in the debate. However, for purposes of understanding the growth of online services, selected interventions are listed here:

- computer-based career guidance and information systems
- vocational assessments and interest inventories
- message boards
- chats
- telephone counseling
- e-mail counseling
- databases
- video and teleconferencing
- combinations of the above interventions

Zunker (1994) described this evolution, including aspects of the debate, by characterizing the career guidance movement as "the story of human progress in a nation founded on the principle of human rights. It touches all aspects of human life, for it has involved political, economic, educational, philosophical and social progress and change" (p. 3). Further evidence of the evolution and expansion of electronic career counseling services and interventions can be observed by the growth of Web sites dedicated to academic career centers and commercial online career services.

ACADEMIC AND COMMERCIAL ONLINE CAREER SERVICES

A brief search of the hard copy and online literature identified more than 1,700 college and university career centers listed on the databases of The National Association of Colleges and Employers (NACE; 1998). Through these more than 1,700 campus services, students, alumni, and interested parties have access to online career services, with many sites encouraging visitors to e-mail questions to staff.

Like the growth of academic career centers, commercial career centers have mushroomed. Dixon (1998) noted "at last count, well over 1,300 employment sites were on the web—and that's a conservative estimate." To help the user know where to start, Dixon identified the top seven career sites, nicknaming them "The Big Seven," and listing their individual attributes.

The Big Seven

1. America's Job Bank (www.ajb.dni.us): for finding state and government jobs.
2. Career Mosaic (www.careermosaic.com): for finding technical and other general jobs.
3. CareerPath.com (www.careerpath.com): one of the best when you're relocating.
4. Espan (www.espan.com): recently renovated and upgraded.
5. Monster Board (www.monster.com): for new graduates and the upwardly mobile.
6. Online Career Center (www.occ.com): high-quality site for seasoned professionals.
7. Yahoo! Classified (classified.yahoo.com/employment.html): for all types of jobs.

Consistent with Dixon's assessment, the *National Business Employment Weekly* (Weddle, 1998) published a special report on "The Best Web Sites for Job Hunters." The report reviewed 70 sites highlighting the best in the following five categories: overall support, job search support, career resources, general purpose use, and specialty use.

Five Best Career Sites for Job Seekers

1. CareerMagazine (www.careermag.com)
2. CareerMosaic (www.careermosaic.com)
3. CareerPath.com (www.careerpath.com)
4. Excite Careers Network (www.excite.com/careers)
5. Online Career Center (www.ooc.com)

Additionally, the report in the *National Business Employment Weekly* selected "the Online Career Center's Magazine, *Career Karma*, with its Career Guru Q & A Column (individualized e-mail career counseling) as the best service for job seekers on the web."

Less than 1 year later, online commercial career centers and Web sites continued to evolve, offering expanded services. For example, The Online Career Center (OCC) and Monster Board merged, expanding services under the new name, Monster.com. Headquartered in Maynard, Massachusetts, Monster.com is considered the leading global careers Web site. Media Metrix, a New York-based company that measures traffic on the Internet, ranked Monster.com as the 71st most visited of all Internet sites. According to a recent report, its ranking was measured by 8.1 million unique visits per month and a network of language sites in the United States, United Kingdom, Australia, Canada, the Netherlands, Belgium, and France. Its newest service, The Talent Market, launched July 4, 1999, provides independent professionals and consultants with a method to market their skills in real time to employers, and speaks to the continuing evolution of new career services via the Web (Time Warner Telecom, Inc., 8/11/99, http://www.prnewswire.com).

The Number One Site

By the end of December 1999, research conducted by Media Metrix for the month of November, reported Monster.com as the number one destination for career seekers and one of the top 100 most visited Web sites overall on the Internet. In December, Monster.com topped off a tremendous year when it announced a 4-year, $100 million relationship with America Online, Inc. (AOL). Under this new agreement, Monster.com (AOL Keyword: Monster) will become the exclusive career search across AOL, AOL Canada, AOL.COM, CompuServe, ICQ, Netscape Netcenter, and Digital City. With more than 20 million members, AOL is the world's leading Internet online service, and its Web brands serve tens of millions of other Internet consumers (Business Wire, 1999).

A review of the online and hard copy literature not only points to the ongoing expansion of Internet career services, it captures concerns surrounding the debate. As noted earlier, the following include: (a) Ethical practice (Can we ensure confidentiality, access?), (b) Client–counselor relationship (How do we protect its integrity against potential misunderstandings arising from a lack of visual clues and what happens in emergencies when the client is halfway around the globe?), (c) Technology (both keeping up with the changes and technology failures), as well as billing and termination issues (What impact do these have on the counseling process?), (d) Research (Because there is virtually no research available, how do we know if online counseling is helpful or harmful?), and (e) Counselor preparation, including certification issues to answer (How can we make a paradigm shift and/or protect the public interest without legislation?).

RESPONSES BY THE STAKEHOLDERS

Given the five issues just outlined, it is my belief that the debate focuses not on whether or not we will have online career counseling, but on the value and efficacy of how this movement continues, including its value to the profession, the individual, and society. Like any debate, the issues articulated in the literature represent various stakeholders. Before discussing my position (first lesson on the road), I offer a closer look at the issues, turning first to (a) leaders in the career development field; (b) providers or vendors of technology and information; and (c) counselors in the trenches.

Leaders in the Field

Differentiating stakeholders starts with a summary of the issues and perspectives articulated by leaders in the field of career development.

Germane to their concerns are comments made by Harris-Bowlsbey, (1996), executive director of the ACT Educational Technology Center and former president of the NCDA, who noted:

> the profession of career counseling is at a crossroads, at a time when its services are more desperately needed than at any other time in history. The structure, that have supported career counseling since its foundation was laid by Frank Parsons, are under attack. If the profession can redesign its structure, theories, and methods of providing services, and if strong, cohesive, national policy and legislation can support those changes, the profession could have a very exciting future. (p. 57)

Like Harris-Bowlsbey, Watts (1996, 1998), an international leader in the field, also viewed the career counseling profession at a crossroads, suggesting that the "explosion of the information technology in general and the rapid expansion of the Internet in particular have huge implications for access to information and to 'distance' career counseling" (Watts, 1996, p. 52). Accordingly, Watts believes that, "Its time (career counseling) has come," noting that it will move forward

> If (career counseling) can demonstrate new forms of adaptability and creativity in its work, it will be able to grasp the opportunity. If it can do so, this could have a powerful contribution to make to the health and prosperity both of our societies and of the individuals within them. (p. 52)

For Harris-Bowlsbey and Watts, the debate is focused on the big picture, the future of the profession, its contributions to society, legislation, and public policy issues.

Vendors and Providers of Services

The second perspective on the debate comes from concerns expressed by technology providers and vendors. Vendors (providers of occupational information and assessment services) see the Department of Labor (DOL) as stepping into their territory. According to Guerra (1998), the DOL traditionally has gathered information that is passed on to career development vendors. The information focuses on occupations and occupational choice. From this information, vendors develop products, which are sold to career counselors and career centers. Currently, vendors are arguing to Congressional officials that this is an antitrust case involving the use of tax dollars by a government agency to compete with private business, versus providing a service to support the business community.

Providers are also concerned that the DOL Web site is being designed without involvement of the career development community. James Sampson, a professor of counselor education at the University of Florida in Gainesville, noted that focus groups are meeting to determine what role the government should play in distributing its information on the Internet. According to Sampson (cited in Guerra, 1998), it is a slow process, with the most important question underlining this facet of the debate being "the ethics of providing these services over the Internet" (p. 22). Accordingly, ethical issues refer to the quality of the information, the question of equal access, and the qualifications of the person delivering the services over the Internet.

Counselors in the Trenches

In contrast to ethical issues focused on the quality of information, the voices of individual career counselors do not appear as vocal as the vendors and leaders, who at times both appear to speak for counselors. Instead, counselors in the psychotherapy camp are the ones articulating the third perspective that focuses on direct service issues or ethical issues about the client–counselor relationship. Sirch-Stasko (1998) described this relationship as "dynamics, which cannot be replicated via the Internet. The spiritual component of what transpires within the therapeutic hour, the non-verbal dialogue, the potential impact … the proximity of counselor to client, are all integral elements of the counseling process" (p. 20). Sirch-Stasko feared by omitting these dimensions that "the very essence of what we do has changed and not for the better" (p. 20).

Others concur with this assessment. For example, Sussman (1998) discussed the loss of the "dialectical process. In face to face counseling there is a continuous and immediate feedback loop between counselor and client. E-mail precludes this … (and) … the complete lack of nonverbal information" (pp. 8, 28). Sussman's assessment is at the heart of the debate for counselors (i.e., that without non-verbal information in a face to face exchange, counseling cannot take place, or at best is compromised). This is consistent with Morrissey (1997) who earlier reported concerns about the:

> difficulty in developing a rapport with someone they've never seen, the absence of body language, clients written communication skills, the expense of keeping up with the latest technology and billing and termination issues. (p. 3)

Sussman also wrote about the pros of online counseling, identifying "some 80 sites where some form of counseling or psychotherapy is purported to occur" (p. 8). Although focusing on mental health counseling, Sussman articulated several advantages that are equally applicable to online career counseling, namely increasing access. She cited four examples of access:

1. Bringing services to underserved populations and geographically isolated areas.
2. Providing increased access to specialists regardless of geographic location.
3. Overcoming transportation problems for people with disabilities or confined to their homes, as well as parents who are restricted by arrangements for leaving work or day-care concerns.
4. Allowing people who are apprehensive about seeking services to do so feeling safe from the confines of their homes.

In contrast Lanning, a professor formerly in the Department of Counseling at the University of Nevada, Las Vegas, and contributor to the NBCC WebCounseling Standards, shared a different view. According to Lanning (cited in Morrissey, 1997), at presentations on the Internet, he regularly asked audiences to suggest principles about online counseling that are different from face-to-face counseling, noting that "No one has identified any yet." Instead, his concern about ethics emphasizes the importance of training and education for counselors who want to offer services via the Internet. He is also concerned about the powerful paternalism that permeates the field. He asked the following:

> If a client is informed about the confidentiality risks of counseling (online or other) why do we think those clients cannot make intelligent informed choices about the Internet as we assume they do in traditional counseling? My office records can be stolen or broken into but we don't worry about that as much as security on the Internet. (p. 3)

MY POSITION IN THE DEBATE

As a private practitioner, I agree with Lanning's observation, that is, more focus should be directed at (a) trusting clients to make informed decisions, (b) recognizing security issues surrounding records may be more fragile in our offices than over the Internet, and (c) emphasizing counselor education and training. Furthermore, I am not surprised that "No one has identified" or suggested principles about online counseling that are different from face-to-face counseling. This is because Lanning's audiences have not been practitioners of the art, which is why I suggest applicable lessons or principles learned from my online practice.

Like other professionals, initially, I suspected the Web would compromise the client–counselor relationship. Yet, after 5 months of immersion in e-mail counseling, my suspicions faded. Instead, my online experiences led me to conclude that the very fears articulated by many professional are just that, fears. Or, if not fears, their concerns may be based on false assumptions about the unknown. The reality of online practice appears to me, and others engaged in its practice to offer several benefits. As observed earlier by Sussman, the most obvious benefit is an increase in access to services by underserved populations. Not as obvious is the added value afforded by the written text and anonymity.

LESSON 1: VALUING WRITTEN TEXTS

As I read the many written messages submitted by clients, and as I further reflected on them, I learned the first of 11 lessons along the road. One of my first observations was noticing that the use of written texts appeared to free clients to ask core questions and, with time for reflection, provided me, the counselor, with rich clues about them and/or their feelings. I speculated that being in the privacy of their own homes with the luxury of remaining anonymous allowed these clients to step forward. At the same time, I observed in their written text clues similar to, if not superior to, those observed during in-person sessions. This meant I was departing from three major assumptions commonly held by counselors "in the trenches" and advocates of face-to-face counseling.

Three Counselor Assumptions

The first of three counselor assumptions I found myself challenging was that visual cues and nonverbal communications are superior to written text. The second was that the counseling process does not take place without visual cues. The third related to the lack of privacy via the Web.

My Rationale

If visual clues are superior to written texts and if the counseling process does not take place without visual cues, then logic suggests that

NBCC and NDCA guidelines, if carried to the extreme, should restrict telephone counseling as a valid modality and restrict the visually impaired from becoming counselors. Both of these restrictions would be considered unthinkable, and surely would spark their own raging debates. Yet, this perspective, coupled with the third assumption or lack of privacy appears to be the underlying logic to restrict career counseling via the Internet.

It is as if proponents of face-to-face counseling cannot envision online messages as nonverbal cues. Nor can they envision the very lack of physical presence as securing another type of relationship, one based on increased privacy, anonymity, and time for reflection. In a culture (the United States) that values visual learning and communication styles, it is perhaps difficult to *see* or value the power of the written word or its nonverbal cues, let alone consider these equally authentic forms of client–counselor communication. Even more difficult, perhaps, is envisioning e-mail or written texts as more authentic forms of dialogue than what happens in the visual moment, particularly, in brief counseling formats. In e-mail counseling, reflection guides the counselor responses, providing time to identify, perhaps, more important cues and implications of the online relationship.

Additional time for reflection may hold the key to help us to make the paradigm shift in how we conduct counseling. For instance, we know emotions, passions, and relationships once were nurtured in written text, as the United States was settled and developed. Throughout U.S. history are examples of diaries, journals, and personal letters (written texts), which remind us how family relationships were enhanced and sustained in times of long separations. If our most cherished relationships can be nurtured via the written word, wouldn't it follow that the counseling relationship could be nurtured in this fashion, too? Couldn't the electronic word allow for both nurturance and access in a way heretofore not acknowledged? Is not the Internet a valuable tool for both access and the development of relationships, even with clients?

Support in the Literature

One of the leaders in the debate may be suggesting this. Writing in *Counseling Today*, Lee (1998), past president of the American Counseling Association, reminded us that:

> We have an emerging generation for whom interaction via the computer is common, natural, and fully accepted means of communication. This

generation of potential clients is used to less actual personal contact and greater interaction in cyberspace in many aspects of their lives. To think that clients in the new century would not expect to access Internet counseling services is probably foolish and shortsighted on our part. (p. 5)

This is consistent with Pietrzak (cited by Morrissey, 1997) who foresees that this issue may become "one of the shifts in paradigms we experience in our profession" (p. 4). Watts (1998) also advocated for a paradigm shift in his keynote at the Seventh Global Conference of the NCDA. Watts observed the following:

We are experiencing a profound revolution in the nature of and structure of work, a revolution that requires new concepts of "career," and ... how career services need to be more extensive than in the past." Thus, he forecast the need to provide, "lifelong access to career counseling ... (in order to provide) ... contributions to the health and prosperity of both individuals and society. (p. 4)

In proceedings and discussions following this NCDA conference, the debate among career counselors appeared far less heated than the debate among counselors in the psychotherapy community. Perhaps this is because NCDA guidelines are highly specific about career counseling practices, which focus on delivery of services versus the deterioration of the client–counselor relationship. Initially, I agreed and shared the concerns of the psychotherapy community, seeing these concerns as directly related to my career counseling practice. At times, I even wondered if computer services might replace my contributions, not to mention compromise my client–counselor relationships.

Support From Face-to-Face Clients

Although hesitant, as more of my clients expressed enthusiasm for online vocational assessments, my concerns diminished, greatly influencing my decision to offer the Myers Briggs Temperament Inventory (MBTI) and Strong Interest Inventory (SSI) via the Internet. This made me the first private practitioner in my city to offer vocational assessment online. With a contract signed through CPP-DB, my enthusiasm for online career services continued as I observed positive benefits and reports from my clients.

Support From the Online Career Center

Once comfortable with assessment online, it was an easy leap in May 1998, when Susan Bryant, product manager for the Online Career

Center (OCC) and Craig Besant, vice president of marketing for OCC, sought my services to launch an online career counseling magazine, *Career Karma*. My role was to write one article per month and answer four to five questions posed by readers. I remember thinking, "With a Q & A feature, this won't last long ... I'll be writing the questions!"

However, the prospect of shaping online services in content and delivery was too enticing to pass up, not to mention working with professionals equally concerned about the ethics and practice of online services. For instance, when I specified the need to follow the NBCC and NCDA WebCounseling Guidelines, there was no problem posting these, nor providing NBCC and NCDA links for referrals and resources.

Support From Online Clients

To my surprise, response to the Q&A feature was overwhelming, more than 250 questions in the first month. Shortly, Netscape requested permission to post one message a day and OCC users sent thank you notes and reports of positive outcomes. When these reports became one in seven, with Netscape drawing 40,000 readers daily, we knew we had touched a nerve.

As questions poured in, I remember thinking "Oh, my gosh, what have I agreed to ... can I fulfill my contract ... how do I prioritize and respond to all these questions?" Of course, this was somewhat rhetorical (or so I thought) as my contract called for me to answer only four to five per month. Yet, faced with more than 250 messages in the first month of operation and the excitement of watching messages arrive, I began to respond personally to the first 40 to 50 questions. I thought this might be a nice gesture. Little did I realize that as I was doing so, the powers that be at the OCC wanted me to answer each one individually, thereby providing a very unique public service, a first of its kind.

After extending our contract to deliver this service, I found myself excited in a way I couldn't remember since I first entered the field by working for Indiana University Purdue University at Indianapolis (IUPUI). There, at the Continuing Education Center for Women (CECW), I provided individual counseling and vocational assessment to a broad base of clients who were seeking educational and vocational direction, career change, career adjustment, and advancement. Because there were few counseling services in the city, then, CECW also provided services to individuals in crisis, people with disabilities, those suffering from substance abuse, and the gay and lesbian community. Some years later, I realized by offering services via the Internet, the excitement I experienced was not only about becoming a trailblazer, it was about providing access to people who otherwise had none. Part of my excitement, too, lay in knowing I was calling on years of experience serving a broad-base clientele as well as drawing on my academic and professional training as a counselor. I knew from the beginning that this work of providing e-mail career counseling looked easy and simple to others. Yet I realized, too, that what made this look easy was my comfort level. My credentials, years of career counseling and life experience, coupled with a deep interest in the global human condition guided my practice. My experience also freed me to observe, speculate, and reflect on insights about this practice, in turn, leading to my second lesson on the road.

LESSON 2: ANONYMITY INCREASES ACCESS

Closely associated with written texts was the role I observed that anonymity played online, that is, anonymity appeared to increase access to services for underserved populations (foreign nationals, people with disabilities, older adults, and those in the gay and lesbian community). In my journal, I recorded my excitement about discovering this medium not as lesser, rather as unique, a kind of adjunct in the same fashion that telephone counseling supports face-to-face counselor–client encounters. Yet, it was much more than telephone counseling. Its very medium offered an added feature. Just as Rogers (1942, 1951) introduced the power of unconditional positive regard and empathy in the client–counselor relationship, departing from the straightforward trait-and-factor approach of Parsons (1909), I began to think of the Internet as holding another departure and new power, the power of anonymity. By providing clients with the opportunity to ask questions anonymously and confidentially, a new type of access was making services available to underserved clients.

Consequently, the very concerns that many counselors express about the Internet creating barriers to the development of the client–counselor relationship may not necessarily be true. The opposite may take place. The medium allows to come forward those clients who previously, out of shame or fear, might have held back. Additionally, those clients in remote locations, people with disabilities, or those worried their questions might appear foolish, were stepping forward everyday. A representative sample of online career counseling clients illustrates these points in the following chapters. Client messages present a closer look at the multiple issues and/or barriers expressed by underserved client populations, with their thank you notes speaking to the effectiveness and benefits of online interventions. Like in-person clients, these online individuals were assured their questions would be answered confidentially, without reference to their names or locations. Even those questions selected for publication in *Career Karma* were posted with respect to their privacy.

SUMMARY

Client examples confirm my position in the debate, that is, like those leaders in the field I believe Internet counseling offers an important contribution for a paradigm shift, particularly for a new generation of clients comfortable online. Examples offered in the following chapters plus another 800 or more online messages, continue to convince me there is not only a need for career counseling via the Web, but that these services can be delivered ethically and confidentially.

In chapters 2 and 3, I continue to address my reflections on practice, articulating additional lessons along the road. For instance, in chapter 2, I define online career counseling, discussing two important career counseling competencies (career counseling theory and individual counseling skills). The chapter elaborates on how to integrate career counseling theory and counselor skills online by identifying nonverbal e-mail cues, and integrating these into counselor responses. Chapter 3 describes the career counseling process, details how to establish and safeguard the client–counselor relationship, and provides examples of issues presented by clients as well as responses to their online questions, thereby developing the value of online career counseling beyond the issue of access.

DISCUSSION QUESTIONS

1. Name the five issues in the debate. Which of these issues is the most relevant for your situation and practice?
2. Which of these five issues is of least concern to you? Why?
3. Which of the three perspectives best describes your job or the role you hope to play in the field of career counseling?
4. In light of the comments and quotes in this chapter, discuss your perspective on the debate, giving support for your view.

2

Defining the Online Career Counseling Process

My interest in the career counseling profession grew from learning the most basic of counseling skills, *active listening*. Active listening is not only listening actively to the content of what a person says, it is listening to the whole person. It means observing nonverbal cues, like gestures, facial expressions, changes in posture, and/or looking for congruence between the nonverbal and verbal messages. Active listening includes listening for the feelings underlining the message, for cultural differences, and/or barriers expressed. By first responding to the sender's feelings, the listener demonstrates what he or she heard, allowing the sender to confirm or correct before new information is added. To be involved with something that comes so naturally, that one does and takes for granted, was exciting to me. Of course, there is more to being a counselor than listening, yet at the time, it was the catalyst for my decision to enter the field. Just as we know few particulars when we fall in love, connecting with a profession, one resonating deep meaning for you, is much the same. Little did I dream then, that one day I would champion active listening as equally important to the online career counseling process.

CAREER COUNSELING COMPETENCIES

Other competencies, such as the 11 listed by the NCDA's (1997a) *Career Counseling Competencies, Revised Version, 1997*, were not as clearly articulated when I was in graduate school in the 1970s, nor were today's certification specialties available for in-depth study. To become a counselor in the 1970s meant becoming a "Jane" of all counseling areas, such as mental health counselor, marriage and family counselor, substance abuse and addictions counselor, school counselor, and my interest area, career counselor. In my state of Indiana, the only specialties requiring additional training were for sexual and/or genetic counseling positions.

Just as counseling competencies crossed specialties then, today's counselors are expected to be knowledgeable not only in their specialty area, they are expected to hold and honor eight competency areas outlined by the American Counseling Association (ACA; 1994) *Code of Ethics and Standards of Practice*. Together, the eight areas recognize the diversity of U.S. society and embrace a cross-cultural approach in support of the worth, dignity, potential, and uniqueness of each individual.

1. The counseling relationship includes promoting the welfare of clients, respecting diversity and client rights, avoiding dual relationships and sexual intimacy, fees, clarifying and discussing termination, and referral; and using computer technology.
2. Confidentiality covers the clients' right to privacy, group and family, minors or incompetent clients, records, research, and training and consultation.
3. Professional responsibility refers to standards of knowledge, professional competence, specialty areas of practice, continuing education, advertising and soliciting clients, credentials, public responsibility, and responsibility to other professionals.
4. Relationships with other professionals covers employers, employees, subcontractors, consultations, and fees for referrals.
5. Evaluation, assessment, and interpretation includes appraisal techniques, competence to use and interpret tests, informed consent, release forms, and test security.
6. Teaching training and supervision.
7. Research and publication.
8. Resolving ethical issues.

In addition to these eight areas, career counselors (those seeking national certification) need to demonstrate additional competency in 11 areas. These are as follows:

1. Career development theory.
2. Individual and group counseling skills.
3. Individual/group assessment.
4. Information resources.
5. Program promotion, management, and implementation.
6. Coaching, consultation, and performance improvements.
7. Diverse populations.
8. Supervision.
9. Ethical/legal issues.
10. Research/evaluation.
11. Technology.

CAREER COUNSELING THEORISTS

Because the career counseling specialty required that a counselor first be knowledgeable about a broad base of general counseling theories, issues, and practices, plus the challenges presented by the world of work, the specialty of career counseling drew me from the start. Career counseling allowed me to work with clients who had diverse backgrounds and who offered a complexity of issues. Later, I would learn the majority of counselors do not share my view, preferring psychotherapy settings to career counseling.

Crites

Pointing to Crites (1981), many in the counseling profession abandoned career counseling in favor of psychotherapy. Although there are many reasons for this phenomenon, Crites noted one of the primary reasons as "the perception of many counseling professionals that career counseling is rather mechanical, straightforward process with little room for creativity or reflection" (p. 16). Furthermore, Crites challenged this perception, suggesting a comprehensive career counseling model that incorporates many theories of counseling and psychotherapy. The model as noted in Sharf consists of the following:

1. The need for career counseling is greater than the need for psychotherapy (a view supported by several surveys).
2. Career counseling can be therapeutic (career and personal adjustment are interrelated).
3. Career counseling should follow psychotherapy (new directions in career development should follow personal adjustment).

4. Career counseling is more effective than psychotherapy (or at least career counseling carries greater expectancy of success than psychotherapy).

5. Career counseling is more difficult than psychotherapy (when career counselors use comprehensive approaches, they are perceived as being both psychotherapists and career counselors).

Sharf

Sharf (1992) built on Crites' views, noting hat many theories of career development are derived from theories of personality. Accordingly, career counseling and psychotherapy theories tend to be a subset of personality theories, utilized "to bring about a desired change in feeling, thinking, or behavior." Sharf stated: "Therefore ... it is natural that counselors who prefer a certain personality theory or theory of counseling are likely to be drawn to a similar theory of career development theory."

Rogers

In my case, Sharf's characterization meant I was drawn to Rogerian theories, or to the nondirective methods, concepts of affective and motivational listening and behavior proposed by Rogers (1942). Self-acceptance and self-understanding were the primary goals of this theory, centered in the client–counselor interaction and relationship, one grounded in mutual respect and directed toward "the client's gaining an understanding of self and taking steps to control his or her destiny" (p.10).

Later Hansen, Stevic, and Warner (1972) summarized Roger's view of client-centered counseling, as an *if–then* approach, emphasizing its goal: "to establish the proper conditions whereby the normal developmental pattern of the individual can be brought back into play" (p. 86). By *if–then* the authors meant that if the following six conditions exist, then the client will gain insight and take positive steps. The client will take control of his or her life and solve his or her difficulties. Thus, the process of counseling can be defined as meeting the following six necessary conditions:

1. Two people must be in contact (Rogers' original word, *relationship*).
2. The client must experience at least a minimum state of anxiety, vulnerability, or in some way be concerned enough to want to make changes.

3. The counselor basically must be an integrated or whole person.
4. The counselor must be present, that is, must be able to have unconditional positive regard toward the client, meaning, the counselor must be nonevaluative about others' worldviews.
5. The counselor has empathic understanding of the client's internal frame of reference.
6. Clients must perceive the counselor's unconditional positive regard for them.

If these six conditions are present, then, according to Rogers' view, the counseling process will take place. Rogers' view of client-centered counseling was considered the first departure from the earliest career development theory formulated by Parson (1909) in his major work, *Choosing a Vocation.*

Parson

Parson's (1909) conceptual framework is a theory based on traits and factors, one that remains popular today. Formulated in three parts, the theory held that career choice and satisfaction occurs when a client's traits or factors are matched with corresponding occupations, by the following:

1. The client has an understanding of self (his or her interests, aptitudes, abilities, limitations, resources and other qualities).
2. The client knows the world of work (requirements and conditions of success, advantages and disadvantages, compensations, opportunities and prospects).
3. The client can reason on the relation between these two groups of facts.

According to Sharf, although Rogers departed from Parson's directive work, later Rogerian concepts were endorsed and integrated into directive counseling, allowing for a broader perspective of human development.

Hansen, Rosberg, and Cramer

Furthermore, Hansen, Rosberg, and Cramer (1994) concluded that if counseling is about providing for the individual's optimum development and well-being, then counselors must "understand as many as possible of the factors that affect people; they must adopt an interdisciplinary approach ... or ... formal eclecticism." An interdisciplinary approach, a formal eclecticism, means understanding both the theory (why) and the process (how) of counseling.

This chapter focuses on the "how" or process of counseling by presenting definitions of career counseling terms as well as my definition of online career counseling. Examples of client–counselor interaction reinforce explanations of the how or process of online career counseling.

THE CAREER COUNSELING PROCESS

So how do Parson's trait-and-factor theories and Rogers' client-centered views apply to today's developmental, behavioral, interdisciplinary, and multicultural approaches to the career counseling process? How do we define the process of online career counseling for counselors, and translate career counseling competencies to online practice? Recent definitions by leaders in the field assist us in the application of skills for online career counseling practice.

Definition by Bloom

According to Morrissey (1997), Bloom, a member of the NBCC Board of Directors and chair of the NBCC Web Counseling Task Force, coined the term *WebCounseling*. Bloom (1997) used the term to define "the practice of professional counseling and information delivery that occurs when client(s) and counselor are in separate or remote locations and utilize electronic means to communicate over the Internet" (p. 1).

Bloom's definition is not inconsistent with definitions offered earlier by Crites (1981), who defined career counseling as a "total-person" approach to counseling. To Crites, career counseling approaches include Parson's trait-and-factor theory (information delivery), Rogers' client-centered and psychodynamic theories (professional counseling), as well as approaches and theories introduced later, such as behavioral, developmental, and cognitive. Crites' integrated or total-person approach to career counseling is consistent with the definition of career counseling offered in the NCDA (1997b) *Guidelines for the Use of the Internet*. The 1997 NCDA document states the following:

> career counseling implies a deeper level of involvement with the client, based on the establishment of a professional counseling relationship

and the potential for dealing with career development concerns well beyond those included in career planning.

Definition According to NCDA

Differentiating between career counseling process and career planning services, the NCDA guidelines note career planning services are limited to providing "information designed to help a client with a specific need." Specific needs are defined as:

> a review of a resume; assistance in networking strategies; identification of occupations based on interests, skills, or prior work experience; support in the job-seeking process; and assessment by means of online inventories of interest, abilities, and/or work-related values.

According to the authors of the NCDA guidelines, the career counseling process goes beyond a specific need, and, as outlined earlier refers to or "implies a deeper level of involvement with the client."

Definition by Guerriero and Allen

Although not writing about the online career counseling process, Guerriero and Allen (1998) defined career counseling as "a process that helps a client address his or her particular career needs" (p. 7). Furthermore these authors defined a process as "a number of sequential steps ... to produce a result ... (and) ... as a way of achieving an output or creating a product." In contrast to Rogers' notion that the client sets the agenda, Guerriero and Allen offered counselors a structured model with specific questions designed to guarantee predictable results. The definition offered by Guerriero and Allen is widely embraced by counselors today, particularly those working in programs where affective domains are not the priority, rather placement in employment or similar measurable outcomes are the determinants for program selection and the continuation of funding sources. Guerriero and Allen's definition is also compatible with the distinction NCDA makes between career planning services and the career counseling process.

Definitions by Sue and Sue

Sue and Sue (1990) challenged the value of traditional insight and behavioral counseling modalities for Third World clients. These authors contended that "many Third World groups who use a different psychosocial unit of operation have different world views that may clash with the world views of White culture and society" (p. 36). Noting that anxiety and confusion may be the outcome for minority clients, Sue and Sue emphasized the necessity for counselors to take the following responsibilities:

1. Become aware of and sensitive to class values and sociopolitical forces impacting the minority client.
2. Understand that culture, class, and language factors can act as barriers.
3. Point out the unique and common experiences related to oppression.
4. Understand culture-bound communication styles.
5. Become aware of one's own racial biases and attitudes.

Definitions by Worell and Remer

Worell and Remer (1992), feminist counselors, also noted omissions in the traditional definitions of the counseling process. These authors point to the definition offered by Herr and Cramer (as cited by Worrell & Remer, 1992): "the total constellation of psychological, sociological, educational, physical, economic, and change factors in combination," adding two important and omitted factors, "sex-role socialization and institutional sexism" (p. 254). Worell and Remer offered an empowerment model for women and minorities to deal with life situations. The model includes "developing a full range of interpersonal and life skills ... (and) ... encourages women to identify and challenge the external conditions of their lives ... that deny them equality of opportunity and access to valued resources" (p. 22).

Definition by Zunker

Zunker (1994) also appeared to acknowledge important omissions from earlier definitions, summarizing the career counseling process as all career choices throughout the life span. Zunker stated: "In the career-counseling process all aspects of individual needs (including family, work, and leisure) are recognized as integral parts of career decision making and planning" (p. 3).

Definitions by Sussman

Sussman (1998) further noted it is important to identify the "means" of "counseling online," stating:

There are two distinct means of Internet counseling. There is the current formulation, which consists mostly of email with some text-based chats, and there is the real time video conferencing of the near future. Although it may not arrive for another two to four years, video and real time audio may make counseling online the "next best thing to being there."

Few definitions on the counseling process discuss "means," perhaps because so few definitions of the online career counseling process exist. Or, because, the greater concern comes from labeling interaction over the Internet by the term, *counseling*. Sirch-Stasko (1998) emphasized that this terminology devalues the very "nature of what we deem to be so special" and "suggests it would be better to frame this communication in a manner that segregates it from counseling per se. Perhaps Cyberspace Consultation would be more fitting" (p. 1).

My Definition

As Sirch-Stasko suggested it is important to distinguish terms. This is a key element in the NCDA Guidelines and an important step in developing my own definition of the online career counseling process.

Working Definition

Just as the NCDA Guidelines distinguished career counseling from career planning services, suggesting career services on the Internet be limited to career planning strategies, I initially concurred. After extensive experience online, I began to believe that although it is important to define terms and make distinctions, who defines the terms is equally important. I believe the definitions and distinctions will be more meaningful when offered at practical levels, or when offered by practitioners of online services. Action research and qualitative approaches hold the promise to define the terminology, bridging this gap and providing useful definitions both for the debate and practice of online counseling.

Testing my Definition

In part, my working definition of career counseling via the Internet began in February 1998, when I was invited to develop and teach a course for the Career Counseling Certification program at the University of California at San Diego (UCSD). In preparation for this program I became acutely aware of issues in the online debate and thoroughly reviewed the various codes of ethics applying to career counselors. These include codes established by the ACA, the NCDA, and the NBCC. Next, I read the written responses to the debate on WebCounseling, the pros and cons offered by the leadership and members of the profession, formulating my own view in the process. Then, at the NCDA's seventh global conference, "Reshaping Career Development for the 21st Century," I listened to national and international leaders discuss the issues, later talking with them and other practitioners in the field. The more I talked with career counseling leaders and practitioners, the more I realized they had no more direct experience online than I. We were talking at theoretical levels. However, in these dialogues and at workshops about online services I found that my intuition was on target about ways to plan for and deliver e-mail career counseling in an ethical and productive manner.

In searching to clarify and define my own perspective on the issues, I immersed myself in the ethics and guidelines of online counseling practice, discovering, in the process, that I had taken the necessary steps to ensure quality services. With my tentative definition adopted from that offered by NCDA or *career planning services* (the delivery of information about a specific need), I felt comfortable forging ahead and did. By becoming the OCC's Career Guru, for 5 months I devoted myself to the full-time practice of e-mail career counseling, answering every e-mail message received daily, including weekends and holidays.

Trusting My Intuition

However, very early into this practice, I found myself questioning the NCDA's definition of online career counseling as *career planning services.* My questions surfaced as I began reading the first 10 to 20 of the 850 or more messages I was to receive as the Career Guru for OCC.com. Few questions, if any, were clear-cut requesting specific information. Examples at the end of the chapter illustrate this point, showing that the questions were more complicated, involving individual and personal circumstances. OCC Staff members, assisting me, noticed this, too, stating that "they (the users/clients) just pour out their hearts!"

Second, I began to realize that my tentative definition ignored everything I knew and held dear from years of practice serving clients. I was reminded, anew, that questions and issues related to careers are very personal, not to mention colored by individual differences related to gender, race, ethnicity, sexual orientation, and physical and mental capacities.

Individual differences are why books on resume writing, job search strategies, and career planning do not answer client questions, and consequently drive clients to career counselors. Clients often say things like, "I've read all the books, but ...." If this is what I know is true for the clients who come to me, "Why on earth," I asked myself, would it be any different for those asking questions online? Deep in my heart, I knew, clients ask what's not in the books. They ask us about attention to their concerns and fears regarding some individual difference or barrier they perceive, whether that be an issue of gender, age, gap in employment, cultural difference, language barriers, physical disability, and on occasion all of the above. To think that online career counseling can be restricted to career planning services, even something that looks as straightforward as reviewing a resume, is like offering a person an ice cream cone, without the ice cream. Who wants it!

An Emerging Definition

In other words, to restrict online career counseling to career planning services is not only difficult, it may be a disservice to the client as well as the profession. Just as I have actively listened to clients in face-to-face sessions, presenting issues and sharing their individual and very personal concerns, so too I found myself listening to online clients. The more messages I read, the more I realized it is difficult, if not impossible, to separate personal issues from career questions, particularly when they are presented by women and minorities. Am I to ignore the heart of their question? If restricted to the NCDA definition of career planning, how, I questioned, do I respond? Early on, I decided, the alternative was to offer an integration model, one based on an in-person counseling model, a total-person approach, feminist model of connection, and, one that included a multicultural perspective.

An integration model would respond to the client questions based on respect for the total person coupled with an understanding and deep respect for the context of their lives and worldviews (Sue & Sue, 1990). It would see clients in the state of becoming (Rogers, 1961), extending an appreciation for their context and connections between peoples (Belenky, Chincy, Goldberger, & Tarule, 1986). Consequently, it became easy for me to redefine my original definition of the online career counseling proves as:

Individualized e-mail career counseling, a specialty of WebCounseling, integrating professional career counseling and career planning services and utilizing electronic resources to communicate and deliver services when the client and the counselor are in separate or remote locations.

What are popularly known as chats, message boards, listserves, or other group activities, sometimes called online career counseling, are excluded from this definition. By definition, these activities are conversational in nature, similar to advisement models used by teachers, librarians, or professional expertise offered via talk radio, television interviews, or newspaper columns.

E-mail, alone, offers a one-on-one experience. E-mail stands for electronic mail. For example, it is a system allowing someone in Aberdeen, Maryland, to communicate quickly and cheaply with someone in Aberdeen, Scotland. According to Dixon (1998) more than 70% of the traffic on the Internet is e-mail, "an electronic tool that transformed the way corporations and small businesses distribute information and conduct their work" (p. 21). E-mail is the method that OCC.com selected for me (Career Guru of its online magazine, *Career Karma*) to respond to the readership, thereby, allowing a global readership to submit questions in an anonymous and confidential manner, receiving individual replies from me, personally, quickly, and at no cost to them.

Like telephone counseling, a one-to-one basis "implies a deeper level of involvement with the client." This means my definition of online career counseling is confined to e-mail career counseling practiced on an individualized, one to one basis, with the e-mail messages and responses written between the client and the career counselor within a specified time frame, similar to individual appointments. The process involves a total person approach similar to that described by Crites (1981). It is a process I define as an integration model, involving both career counseling modalities, career planning services, including information and referrals or links to services specific to client questions, and with an appreciation for the client's context, worldviews, and connections between peoples.

LESSON 3: CAREER COUNSELING IS PERSONAL COUNSELING

As outlined in chapter 1, my first two lessons taught me the following:

1. Reflection on written texts can be as powerful as visual cues.
2. Anonymity increases access to underserved populations.

Just as these first two lessons were drawn from reflection about online practice, I discovered a third lesson: It is difficult, if not impossible, to separate career issues or questions from personal issues. Career counseling is personal counseling, whether it is offered in person or online, further leading me to view online career counseling as a specialty of WebCounseling. I base my conclusions on both actual practice delivering online services and from studying and reflecting on the issues in the debate literature related to online counseling. Furthermore, my conclusions are grounded in years of experience as a practitioner of career counseling services. From both experiences (online and in-person), I propose the following three points regarding career counseling as personal counseling:

1. Separating personal issues from career information is difficult, if not impossible.
2. Responding to career issues online is not that different from responding in person. One must still acquire similar skills, attitudes, knowledge, and respect for various worldviews.
3. Approaching career counseling based on the theories of Rogers, Crites, Sue and Sue, and others can be delivered ethically, professionally, and with positive outcomes.

To me, the definition of WebCounseling coined by Bloom (1997) refers to both personal and career counseling, additionally including information and/or referrals specific to client questions. This means an online career counselor must first be skilled at active listening to client messages. Just as counselors who meet with clients face-to-face must *read* nonverbal cues in clients' facial expressions or behaviors, the online counselor needs to be skilled at actively listening and reading in between the lines of written texts to reflect on the written message.

EXAMPLES OF CAREER COUNSELING AS PERSONAL COUNSELING

Here are four examples illustrating an integrated approach to online career counseling. The examples incorporate the first three lessons learned along the road: reflection on written texts, increased access, and career counseling as personal counseling requiring an integrated approach.

Example 1: Recent College Graduate

A young man writes about graduating from college, switching jobs three times, asking four questions: Is it too soon to look? Will I need to pay back my company for relocation costs? Is it totally crazy ...

> I graduated from college just a little over a year ago and have already switched jobs 3 times. The first job I took out of school turned out to be a complete disaster. The company relocated me from Cleveland to Dallas and my contract stated that if I left before a year, I would owe all the relocation expenses back. I was lucky enough to find a job in Los Angeles 9 months later that I loved. Most of my family and friends were in S. California so it worked out great. In addition, the company picked up my tab for relocation from Dallas to LA and paid back the money I owed to the company in Dallas for my move from Cleveland to Dallas. Unfortunately, I was laid off 5 months later. I was unable to find another job in my field in LA so I reluctantly took a job in Chicago for fear of not being able to pay my rent! The company in Chicago paid for my relocation and I was excited about the opportunity.
>
> However, all is not well. I've been at the new position for a month and I can't stand it. My job function is completely different from what I originally agreed to. I mentioned this to my boss but he told me the offer letter clearly stated "and other duties as assigned." I fear the work I am doing now will not help me in my future career at all. The tasks I perform are meaningless. I had more responsibility as an intern. Since I have jumped so much and it is so early in my career, would it be too soon to start looking? Also, if I left now I would owe the Chicago company back all the relocation costs from my move. Is it totally crazy to think someone would be willing to provide the same kind of package as I found in LA? I desperately want to go back to S. California and get back to my normal life. My biggest fear is that my resume will read as if I am a professional drifter. I appreciate you taking the time to read my letter. Thank you.

As may be noted, this student's questions are straightforward. Yet, he chooses words and phrases like "complete disaster," "unfortunately laid off," "reluctantly to pay rent," "meaningless tasks," "desperately want to go back," and biggest fear ... "professional drifter," suggesting he may be worried, anxious, scared to make a mistake, perhaps too stuck to take another risk. So, how does the Web counselor respond? Does he or she ignore what might be considered strictly counseling issues and provide only career information? Or, does the counselor follow Rogerian concepts (i.e., fostering a climate of trust and affirmation by normalizing client feelings, followed by the integration of client feelings with pertinent career information)? You decide. Here's what I wrote:

> Some experts say the best time to look for a job is right after you've accepted one. So by all means start looking and don't worry about being a professional drifter. No one will think that when they learn you were wooed to accept better offers from each employer. And, you're not crazy to think someone might be willing to provide a similar package to yours in LA. If it happened once, it can happen again. Many companies have sign-on bonuses, which are traded for relocation costs or vice versa. Whether you will owe your current company back costs is something you'll need to ask them. You might want to ask, beforehand, about the company's policy on probationary periods. If there is one, job responsibilities may be evaluated at that time. Things do change. Before leaving do all you can to make this position work for your sake and theirs. As you do this, you'll be bringing closure and leaving because of a conflict of values, with your heart in California. No one can fault you for that either. Good luck and keep me posted.

Here is the client's reply to my message. The speed of his reply indicates that a whole-person approach reduced his anxiety. The tone of his second message also suggests he is no longer feeling stuck, rather free to focus on new options.

> I honestly can't thank you enough for your advice. I feel so much more relaxed about my career situation and potential options now. Take care. Again, my sincerest thanks

Example 2: A Foreign National

The second example also shows the importance of paying attention to tone. Like counselors in face-to-face sessions, the Web counselor needs to pay attention to the tone of the e-mail message, that is the language chosen, the feelings expressed (i.e., enthusiasm or a lack of, fear, sadness, discouragement, pain, etc.). And, just as these feelings are not always clear in a face-to-face encounter, they are not always clear on the printed page. As counselors, it is our job to check out the meaning behind the client's words, whether in person or on paper. Here's an example of a client asking a straightforward question, identifying his problem as one of "mobbing." Yet, is it so straightforward, how would you respond?

I'm facing with the mobbing problem. There are several scientific companies using the method to influence peoples (I mean, at least Russian companies). Could you reveal possible ways to avoid that? The problem arise from time to time, independing on chiefs (technicks and technologies). Is it the way to do science on the world, indeed? Thank you in advance for any advice.

Before answering this message, I spent some time trying to identify the word *mobbing*. What did this mean? Did it refer to the Russian gangs reported by the news media? And, what did "independing on chiefs," mean, or "do science on the world?" Was the writer referring to bomb threats? Or was this a case of a language barrier or cultural differences in expressing written concerns? I also spent time reflecting on the best way to reply. Finally, I decided I had forgotten a primary counseling technique: when in doubt, check it out. Consequently, I did what I would do in any face-to-face session, I asked the client to clarify:

I am not familiar with the term mobbing or a mobbing problem. If you would like to clarify or write another question, I will be happy to reply.

The client quickly restated his original question. Obviously, he was not writing about Russian gangs or bomb threats. His clarification and speedy response serve to demonstrate the importance of paying attention to client clues for cultural and language barriers. In his return message he shows both appreciation and respect for my responses, writing ...

Dear career guru!
I've considered your work as very useful to everyone. What can I say about mobbing? There is a German psychologists term which appeared recently. Mobbing means psychological (and another) pressing (usually with respect to just employed peoples or active peoples in the conservative companies) to force peoples leaving their jobs (often under terrible psychic conditions). There are many peoples, who lost their healthy, not to mention jobs, felt victims to mobbing. Unfortunately, I haven't a book about it, but I've read it. If I'll remember the authors, I'll inform you. Thank you for your carry about peoples. I hope you recognize the mobbing with too little information submitted for you.

With clarification from the client, I then responded by both affirming him (the counseling component) and providing information resources and links for managing stress as well as a list of healthy companies (the career planning component).

> Yes, I understand now what you mean by mobbing. We might call it downsizing, high stress on the job. The only way I know to avoid it, is to research a company well, before you interview there. Then you need to be very observant in your interview and ask questions, which will help you determine the pros and cons of the company. Interviewing this way will help you determine if the company will be a healthy environment for you. One resource on the health of companies is The Wellness Councils of America. This organization has compiled a list of companies by State that have been identified as healthy. You can read more about these companies as well as how to handle stress in this month's issue of Career Karma at: http://www.careerkarma.com/199810/02/. On this site, you'll find the other Career Karma articles of interest. Thank you for your kind words and I hope this information helps.

Example 3: Downsized Female Employee

In the following message, the writer makes a statement instead of asking a question.

> I was just released from the company that employed me for over 55 months. I received outstanding reviews and pay increased of better than 15% each year. I am having a difficult time understanding the rational behind the firm's choice of personnel to release.

What is important in this statement? Is she hurt? Confused? Does she need help finding a new position? What is she asking and how should a Web counselor respond? Sometime, the best clue for an appropriate response is the response you might give in a face-to-face session. In the following response, I begin with an acknowledgment and affirmation that the situation is hard to understand, followed by a pacing technique, or stating the following message in a factual manner, similar to the tone of her message. I use this tone to point out that business decisions reflect the company's bottom line, not an individual's worth. Noting, too, that it might be difficult to learn from this and move on, a link is offered for contacting a certified career counselor. Although I considered other suggestions, I decided to keep this message simple because there wasn't a clearly stated question. What would you have written? Here is the response:

> Yes, it is hard to understand! Unfortunately it happens and generally has nothing to do with your contributions. Keep in mind, this was a business decision rather than a statement about you. And, the decision has to do with the company bottom line rather than your skills or personal worth. The best thing is to learn from this and move on. If it's too difficult, meet with a qualified career counselor who can help you sort things and develop action plans. To contact a career counselor in your area check with the National Board of Certified Counselors at: http://www.nbcc.org. Take care. Sincerely, The Career Guru

Example 4: African-American Female, Career Changer

In the following message, the writer expresses several concerns: age (she is too old to start anew), work history (technical vs. the creative side of her industry), and not knowing where to turn or begin. Yet she appears optimistic. She writes

> Dr. Pat:
> I am a 35 yr old African-American female. I have a Bachelor's degree in Public Relations & Advertising. I'm also an experienced voice-over artist. My dilemma is this: A love for writing and speaking and being on camera or onstage, and a love for communicating with children in particular. A little experience in & love of modeling. The catch? I've spent the past 10 years, since graduating college, in the television industry (behind the camera, on the technical side). Now, it seems, no one will give me the opportunity to prove that I am indeed a strong writer as well as a natural on-air talent. Please, can you help me? Any career suggestions will be greatly appreciated. I'm afraid I'm nearing the point where employers will consider me too old for consideration in any entry-level position. I don't know where else to turn. Thank you for your time. Sincerely, Cautiously Optimistic'

Because she signs her message, "Cautiously Optimistic," I interpret this to mean she is expressing hopefulness, not necessarily observed in the tone of the previous message. All the same, hers is a highly competitive field and this fact needs to be acknowledged, justifying the need for a little help, which is how the response begins. Because she is hopeful, chances are she is in a position to hear and receive concrete information, such as suggestions to contact professional organizations or to participate in volunteer activities. If the tone of her letter had indicated great discouragement, she might not be ready to hear these suggestions or link to the Web site provided at the end of the response. To verify these assumptions, I ask for feedback at the end of the message. Here is what I wrote:

> This is a tough situation because your field is so competitive. However, you're not too old. You just need a little help. Sometimes you can get this by networking within the industry or through professional associations like the local chapter of the American Federation of Television and Radio Artists. Or you might consider signing up for an internship or volunteering at a PBS Station that focuses on children's programming. What you may need most is a strong mentor or agent to help you. Have you looked at sites like Thomas E. Bliss & Associates: http://www.etbliss.com/. Let me know if this helps. Sincerely, The Career Guru

Asking for feedback is an equally important part of this message. It is only with the client's acknowledgment that assumptions about tone, feelings, and appropriate information can be determined. In this case, the assumptions were all on target and the information was received as helpful, particularly because this time she signed her name, a signal of sincerity.

> Thanks for responding. I appreciate it. This helps immensely. I'll give the "etbliss" site a try. Your help is greatly appreciated.

SUMMARY

These examples from actual practice are offered to demonstrate e-mail career counseling as an integration model, which combines career counseling skills and career planning services, with attention to other worldviews. I believe the examples also demonstrate client issues and feelings about the service indicating e-mail counseling can be conducted ethically, appropriately, and professionally.

Furthermore, the examples serve to illustrate the complexity of skills needed to respond effectively online. In addition to career counseling skills and knowledge of career planning services, adjunct skills are needed. Adjunct skills begin with reflection on the client's message and include a computer comfort level to respond online by utilizing search engines and databases to identify appropriate resources. Adjunct skills also mean writing and editing skills, not to mention organizational ability to juggle responses by prioritizing, analyzing, toggling online, cutting and pasting, editing, and rereading before sending. Tracking and sorting into folders, reflecting again, and sometimes rewriting, and/or asking for client feedback are other adjunct skills necessary for e-mail career counseling.

In the next chapter, Safeguarding the Client–Counselor Relationship, ethical issues regarding confidentiality are covered, including the power of anonymity. The chapter also discusses the fourth lesson from the road, the importance of listening to client voices in safeguarding the client–counselor relationship. Five themes revealed in client voices demonstrate the client's view of confidentiality both in the online career counseling process and in safeguarding the client–counselor relationship.

DISCUSSION QUESTIONS

1. Discuss and prioritize the 11 career counseling competencies, noting why knowledge of these is important to the practice of in-person and online career counseling.
2. Name three career counseling theorists and discuss why their views are important to practice, stating which one best describes or does not incorporate your views.
3. State and discuss your personal theory of the career counseling process, in-person and online.
4. In the examples of clients presented, how would you prioritize their needs? Whose questions should be answered first? Why or why not?
5. Do you agree or disagree with the responses to client questions? How would you have responded? What would help you to formulate a better response?

3

Safeguarding the Client–Counselor Relationship

For counselors, the heart of the debate about online counseling is safeguarding the client–counselor relationship. Concerns center on integrity, how to protect the relationship against potential misunderstandings arising from a lack of visual clues, and how to ensure confidentiality over the Internet. Interestingly as cited in Morrissey (1997), Lanning reminded us at presentations he gives on the Internet when he asks audiences to suggest principles about online counseling that are different from face to face, he found: "No one has identified any yet." Is there a difference? Searching for answers led to my fourth lesson on the road: listening to client voices.

SAFEGUARDING ONLINE IS THE SAME AS IN-PERSON

Because little research has been conducted on safeguarding the online client–counselor relationship, evidence to inform us is sparse. However, Lanning's observations suggest there is little difference. If this is so, perhaps we have lost sight of the simple answer to these concerns. Simply, we safeguard online relationships in the same manner that we safeguard in-person counseling situations. We ensure confidentiality over the Internet by being good professionals, following best practices, and becoming good people in daily life.

This means we need to be knowledgeable about the theory and practice of counseling, adhere to ethical standards and practices, and keep current with changes and additions to our respective codes. Additions include the standards for online counseling and career services recently approved by NBCC and the NCDA.

Like most counselors, I take seriously, the mandate to "do no harm" and "promote the general welfare" of clients. Yet, in everyday practice, I only spend time examining the various codes of ethics when there's a perceived problem or dilemma. Certainly, this was true in my search for guidance regarding online standards. In the process I rediscovered how many answers and guidelines for practice can be found among our codes.

NBCC Standards for Ethical Practice

I was fortunate to look for answers when the NBCC standards were first published. The document begins by emphasizing, "This document, like all codes of conduct, will change as information and circumstances not yet foreseen evolve ... (and) ... are not to duplicate non-Internet-based standards adopted in other codes of ethics." The statement indicates counselors, first and foremost, are to follow the standards for in person counseling as they practice counseling online. Thus, the 13 NBCC guidelines are extra standards to follow. Four of the 13 are particularly pertinent to the discussion of safeguarding the relationship and/or to confidentiality:

1. To inform clients about the security of client/counselor/supervisor communications and potential hazards of unsecured communications on the Internet (Guideline 2).
2. To mention presenting problems inappropriate for WebCounseling, providing specific examples (Guideline 11).
3. To explain to clients the possibility of technology failure (Guideline 12).
4. To explain how to cope with potential misunderstandings arising from the lack of visual clues from the WebCounselor or Web client (Guideline 13).

NCDA Guidelines for Use of the Internet

In contrast to NBCC WebCounseling Guidelines, NCDA Guidelines are specific to career services. NCDA Guidelines emphasize the delivery of information, such as the qualifications of the website developer/provider versus career counselor qualifications (Guideline 1); the importance of using previously tested databases and computer-based career information and guidance systems (Guideline 3); and the use of online assessment (Guideline 8, a–e). However, like the NBCC document, the NCDA Guidelines stress adherence to the same codes for face-to-face counseling sessions. For example, in discussing the use of online assessment, NCDA states:

- The counselor must abide by the same ethical guidelines as if he or she were administering and interpreting these same inventories or tests in face-to-face mode and/or in print form (Guideline 8, b).
- Every effort must be exerted to protect the confidentiality of the user's results (Guideline 8, c).
- If there is evidence that the client does not understand the results … by email or telephone interchanges, the counselor must refer the client to a qualified career counselor in his or her geographic area (Guideline 8, d).

FORMING MY THEORY OF ONLINE PRACTICE

When I sought answers beyond NBCC and NCDA guidelines, I noticed the absence of client voices. In the literature, there was no mention of their thoughts. Nor had researchers chronicled what users of online services had to say about safeguarding the relationship. Professionals appeared to hold one of two views. Either they referred to the authority figures (my tendency) to define web guidelines or standards of delivery, or they believed independently that they know what is best for clients. The third alternative was not apparent in the literature, that is, asking clients (the partners in this relationship) how they would define safeguarding the relationship. Instead of soliciting client input for insight or clues, professionals appeared to adhere to the tradition that says, "they (clients) speak with their feet," or they tell what they want or need by seeking, continuing, and/or declining services.

Speaking With Their Feet

Speaking with their feet is one of the ways professionals measure the importance of an issue, a new perspective, or an emerging specialty. For instance, when clients come forth in large numbers seeking help with a specific problem, we pay attention. In the process we create strategies to meet the demand. In turn, this leads to the development of counselor competencies. Developing competencies creates and increases the need for counselor programs or continuing education workshops about specific issues. From these programs, new specialties emerge. This is the process or life cycle of NBCC specialty credentials such as the credentials for National Certified Career Counselors (NCCC), Master Addictions Counselor (MAC) and National Certified School Counselors (NCSC) to name three. In reverse, the same rational, speaking with their feet, applies. Take the recently retired NCCC. It was born to meet a growing demand, then retired in June 1999. NBCC sited two reasons: the decline in applications, and the expense to maintain the specialty.

Whether initiating or retiring a specialty, speaking with their feet is not a bad measurement; it's just not the only one. Perhaps this tendency is what underlies Lanning's (as cited in Morrissey, 1997) concern about "a paternalism that permeates the field" (p. 3). Although paternalism can be an issue in organizations and certainly is related to this discussion, it is secondary to this study. Yet, understanding the role of paternalism led to my fourth lesson on the road, listening to and honoring client voices.

LESSON 4: LISTENING TO CLIENT VOICES

Client voices demonstrate and provide important lessons for us all, particularly about counseling via the Internet. I believe, too, if we are to satisfactorily answer how we safeguard the online client–counselor relationship, the response needs to include client voices. We need to ask clients directly or at the very least pay attention to the clues they provide. Looking back, several steps led me to this conclusion. These steps were not necessarily linear. Many happened simultaneously including reflecting on practice, identifying client themes, talking with experts, and reviewing various ethical codes. Often, I found myself reflecting on practice while I reviewed various ethical codes, made journal notes, listened to client messages. Many times, too, while searching for answers online, in journals, or even talking with experts, I reflected on practice. Because reflection on practice permeates everything I do as a researcher and counselor, I start with reflection on practice as the first indicator regarding the importance of client voices.

Reflecting on Practice

August 1999 marked my first year anniversary as an online career counselor. Yet, I hardly noticed, until mid-September when I opened a letter from a prospective client who wrote simply,

> Dear Dr. Boer:
> After reading about you on Monster.com, I wanted to write you immediately. I need some help finding direction in my life and career ... I am 32 years old, have a Bachelor of Arts ... my biggest problem is ... (and) ... deciding what I should do next ... you may call me either during the day or in the evening.

By including phone numbers and times to reach her, like others, this client revealed her readiness for career services. The simplicity of this letter made me realize how I had become accustomed to online services, taking for granted my growing respect of the medium. It also jolted my realization that I have grown accustomed to receiving daily messages.

Observing the Numbers.   Starting as the online Career Guru for OCC.com, I had answered 850 or more messages in 5 months. After the merger with Monster, an equal number of clients continued to contact my private practice by e-mail, phone, and letter, while a new population of more than 3,000 clients wrote the Career Guru Message Board. Together there were 4,700 individuals seeking career services. By any tally that's an impressive number, particularly when it represents pleas to only one career counselor. These more than 4,700 clients represent a growing and global population for which safeguarding the client–counselor relationship is equally important. Their numbers alone reveal a need for online career counseling. That's why I believe the question of how to safeguard this special relationship is one of the most important issues in the debate. It speaks to the very heart of what we do as counselors: how we interact with clients. If we fail to answer this question, we fail. I believe, too, that if we cannot define satisfactorily how we safeguard the relationship in person settings, we won't have a clue about safeguarding it online. Safeguarding is more than a technical problem of securing log on names and passwords.

Broadening the Scope.   Initially, I viewed the concept of safeguarding the client–counselor relationship as technical in nature, equating it with online security breeches. I suspect I am not the only counselor who started there. If you are not actively online with clients, it's a logical conclusion. However, once I began searching for answers, I discovered the American Library Association (ALA) has addressed this issue for two decades. In the publication, *Bill of Rights and Responsibilities for the Electronic Community of Learners* (January 23, 1980), the ALA emphasizes personal responsibility for both individuals and institutions, stating in its preamble:

> As technology assumes an integral role in education and lifelong learning, technological empowerment of individuals and organizations becomes a requirement and right for students, faculty, staff, and institutions, bringing with it new levels of responsibility that individuals and institutions have to themselves and to other members of the educational community.

According to the ALA, individual responsibility means that citizens are responsible for all other citizens. It is our job "to respect and value the rights of privacy for all; to recognize and respect the diversity of the population; to behave ethically; and comply with legal restrictions regarding the use of information resources" (Article II. 4).

Identifying Pertinent Policies.   Since the early 1990s many school districts have struggled with similar questions of access and ethics, particularly as they prepared to bring connectivity into the schools. According to Wolf, (1994) the "easy" questions deal with technical issues: "How does one connect?" or "Who will offer the service and how much does it cost?" The tougher questions are: "Is it worth the cost?" and "What do we do when one of the students accesses information which is racist, sexist, sexually explicit or objectionable in some other way?" To address these issues, Wolf pointed to Acceptable Use Policies (AUP), warning:

> Parents and children should not post personal information such as name, address, or phone number. Users are warned that their account is theirs and they should protect it - that is, don't let others use it, don't tell people your password, and follow safe password practices such as frequent changes and non-word choices. (p. 17)

Wolf also cited the importance of training and compliance with acceptable use behaviors pointing to draft policy statements of the Waiakea Intermediate School, Hilo, Hawaii: "Waiakea will require all such users to be trained in 'Netiquette,' Electronic Communication Ethics and User Responsibilities" (p. 24).

Clearly, public school systems and libraries have dealt with and have increased public awareness about appropriate use of the Internet. Training in user responsibility, netiquette, and ethics lays the groundwork for best practices in the counseling field. This means that safeguarding the client–counselor relationship includes user responsibilities coupled with counselor responsibilities for best practices, biases, and how these are handled. Safeguarding means knowing and keeping current with our evolving professional codes of ethics. To this list of best practices I add that safeguarding also means listening to clients.

Identifying Client Themes

Listening to my clients first prompted me to explore online services. Clients regularly asked about online assessments, wondering when I would offer these and why or why not? They would state how convenient it would be to complete assessments from their homes, not to mention the ability to contact me by e-mail when they had questions. In the beginning, I was hesitant.

As I searched for answers, growing numbers of clients contacted me over the phone, by mail, and through OCC.com. Messages arrived daily not only from the United States, but from more than a dozen countries including Burma, Austria, Canada, China, Ghana, Holland, India, Italy, Mexico, Nigeria, Pakistan, Russia, Switzerland, Thailand, Sweden, Venezuela, and the United Kingdom. Whether by e-mail or letter, whether from international or U.S. clients, each message started similarly to the letter noted earlier. They began with phrases referring to my credentials, such as: "I read your credentials on Monster.com," "Because of your extensive experience," "After reviewing your bio I feel you have the qualifications to assist me," or simply, "I've been looking for someone like you to help me."

After reading several hundred messages beginning in a similar fashion, it was easy to conclude credentials are an important part of the equation for those seeking online help. In fact, credentials appeared to be more important than the issue of confidentiality. Few messages noted fear of disclosure. If confidentiality was important, these same clients requested it: "please keep this confidential," or "I'm writing you because I want this kept confidential," and/or "please send replies to my home e-mail or phone number rather than my work address." By reflecting on recurring phrases in the client messages, I began to observe three recurring themes with implications for safeguarding the client–counselor relationship from the clients' perspective.

Theme 1: Counselor Credentials. Clients write or tell me they believe I can help them because they have read my credentials and/or about my experience in the field. My biography is posted online for clients to review, a practice consistent with *WebCounseling Guidelines for Counseling Over the Internet.* In this way, clients may read where I earned my undergraduate as well as graduate degrees and in which disciplines. They are able to learn which certifications I have earned, positions I have held, clients I have served, and my membership affiliations. In the section stating I am a member of the NCDA and certified by the NBCC, links are provided to both organizations. By clicking on these links, clients may read the Ethical Standards I follow for providing career counseling over the Internet. These same links provide access to consumer guidelines for selecting a career counselor as well as client rights and responsibilities. In this way, too, clients know ahead of time exactly what services are provided, for whom the services are provided, and what my credentials are. This information appears to give online clients a sense of trust, security, and an invitation to seek services. Armed with the pros and cons, they are free to make their choices about the merits of using online career counseling services.

Theme 2: Trust. The sheer numbers of people seeking online services suggest that limitations regarding visual clues and confidentiality are not clients' primary issues. When they are, clients make requests trusting these will be honored. Otherwise, they appear comfortable online, perhaps due to prior experience at schools, in libraries, or from training sessions on netiquette, or even from reading privacy statements. Contrary to warnings, the majority of clients plunge ahead, posting questions including personal data, sharing their first and last name, age, marital status, educational level, and profession. Some include phone numbers. By reading the privacy statement and then using the service, clients agree to the terms or limitations of privacy and in effect waive their rights. This is consistent with ACA's (1994) *Code of Ethics,* "The right to privacy may be waived by the client or his or her legally recognized representative" (Section B: Confidentiality, b.).

Knowing this, it is astonishing to me that of the more than 4,700 messages I received in 1 year, I would not consider one a crank, obscene, nor even testy. Rather the messages are well written, expressed with sincerity, and arrive from educated professionals, with equal numbers holding undergraduate, graduate, and professional degrees. Their tone is serious. Some give more details than others, yet nearly all reveal personal data beyond informational questions defined by NCDA as "a specific need, such as review of a resume."

Instead of asking informational questions like: "What's the difference between a chronological and functional resume?" The writers ask, "What's the best resume to write in my circumstances?" Often, circumstances are expressed as fears, including house husbands, who are fearful of re-entering the job market, clients fired or downsized, women re-entering the market following divorce or the death of a spouse, and professionals wanting a career change. A large number come from foreign nationals and still others from people with disabilities. A much smaller number represent the gay and lesbian communities, who present discrimination issues related to their job search. Regardless of issue, each group expresses personal motivation for career change exceeding that of clients' in-person sessions.

Theme 3: Appreciation.   One of the most convincing reasons to believe clients have something to say about trust and confidentiality is their appreciation. Thank you notes (one in seven) demonstrate not only appreciation for this medium of delivery, the messages show they receive more than answers to a "specific need." And, they write knowing their messages may be made public. These messages demonstrate that confidentiality, privacy if you will, is more of a concern for the counselor than for the client. Consider these:

- I honestly can't thank you enough for your advice. I feel so much more relaxed about my career situation and potential options now.
- Thank you for responding to my message. Your input has given me insight on how I should handle the issue and myself. You are a true help. Thank you.
- For many months I had been searching for an answer on a rather difficult subject. I queried many sources both on and off the net; with no result. My inquiry was answered [by CareerGuru] in an impressive turnaround time—which is a nice touch in itself. More important, the advice dealt specifically with what I wanted to know and pinpointed the direction (complete with addresses)

most advantageous to my goal. In simpler terms Watson .... It's the best thing since sliced bread. Oh, one more thing. It's free.

- Thank you career guru. You are a real GURU! Your answer gave me a peace of mind I won't forget. I will keep you posted. Thanks again.
- Patricia: thanks a lot for your information it helped me getting some grip. I will keep you informed how things are working out for me and I might also bother you with some further questions.
- Thank you so much for responding so quickly. I do have a strong support network and that has certainly helped me over the last few months. I do agree that it's time to consult a career counselor. I had access to one back in the summer, however, did not feel she was much support. She didn't offer much encouragement ... it's time to find someone who can be supportive!
  Thanks again!!!

These examples offer additional insights beyond appreciation. Consider the following:

1. Language. Notice in each message that the individual thanks me for more than information. Each uses affective phrases like, "feeling more relaxed," "giving me insight," "finding specific answers," "giving me peace of mind," "gaining a grip," and, "time to find someone who can be supportive!" Isn't this counseling language?

2. Client Movement. In face-to-face sessions, we watch for client movement by observing what clients do and say (i.e., facial expressions, body language, suggesting positive change).Client movement is about observing a client in distress who is showing behavioral signs of resolution, readiness for change, and/or congruence between their language and behavior. These thank you messages clearly indicate client movement

3. Format. Appreciation for online formats is also apparent in two ways. First, it is stated in phrases like: "an impressive turnaround time—which is a nice touch in itself," "responding so quickly," and "one more thing. It's free." Second, an appreciation for the format is implied in the message itself. One out of seven clients take time to write these messages. How many in-person clients write their counselors when they gain insight, feel more relaxed, have peace of mind, or appreciate turnaround time?

4. Ethical Concerns. Is there anything in these thank you examples that comes close to violating ethical codes or standards of prac-

tice? Do any clients express distress that their confidentiality or security has been violated? What would the experts say?

Talking With Experts

Before practicing online, before reading *the Standards for Ethical Practice of WebCounseling* (NBCC, 1997, 1999), I sought answers to ethical concerns by calling the ethics committee at the ACA. My early questions centered on confidentiality issues related to online assessment. As the representative answered my questions, he referred several times to the ACA *Code of Ethics*, citing specific section numbers for my review. Once assured that properly administering the online assessment would not compromise the confidentiality of my clients, I talked with the test providers at CPP-DB. From them I learned only those licensed to purchase assessment instruments could be licensed to provide assessments online.

Furthermore, the public cannot just go online and link to CPP-DB, taking any instrument they choose. The client must first contact a certified counselor who determines the appropriateness of the instrument for the client. Once that determination is made, the client is given instructions along with a logon name and password. Nor can the client print the results. Only the counselor has access to the printed results. In other words, the testing company was observing standards compatible with and outlined in the ACA *Code of Ethics* regarding safeguards for the ethical administration of online assessment instruments.

I followed this same process regarding confidentiality issues related to e-mail career counseling. In addition, I discussed liability insurance issues with ACA representatives and increased my coverage. I also learned the importance of informing clients of encryption methods used to help ensure the security of the online communication. In my work with OCC.com and Monster.com, encryption methods were used whenever possible, with the hazards of unsecured communication fully explained, as well as a full explanation of what is appropriate and inappropriate for online career counseling messages.

Reviewing Various Ethical Codes

While talking with the experts and leaders in the field, I also reviewed the relevant code of ethics. As a NCCC, three professional associations support my practice: the ACA, the NCDA, and the NBCC.

In addition, these three organizations make available other resources to guide my practice and to help inform about safeguarding the client–counselor relationship. ACA offers the *Practitioner's Guide to Ethical Decision Making*, NBCC provides the *Standards for the Ethical Practice of WebCounseling*, and the NCDA publishes the *Guidelines for the Use of the Internet for Provision of Career Information and Planning Services*.

American Counseling Association

According to the ACA *Code of Ethics and Standards of Practice*, "a code enables the association to clarify to current and future members and to those served by members, the nature of the ethical responsibilities held in common by its members." The ACA *Code of Ethics* includes eight sections with eight respective standards of practice, representing minimal behavioral statements. These are:

1. The counseling relationship
2. Confidentiality
3. Professional responsibility
4. Relationships with other professionals
5. Evaluation, assessment, and interpretation
6. Teaching, training, and supervision
7. Research and publication
8. Resolving ethical issues.

Although all eight are important for the practice of counseling, three are particularly pertinent to a discussion on safeguarding the client–counselor relationship: the counseling relationship, confidentiality, and resolving ethical issues.

The Counseling Relationship. Section A of the code begins with a clear statement that the client's welfare is the primary responsibility of the counselor. This means the counselor is "to respect the dignity and to promote the welfare of clients," and "to encourage client growth and development." Twelve subsections of Section A outline responsibilities to ensure the clients' welfare, including Computer Technology (A.12.): use of computers, explanation of limitations, and access to computer applications in counseling services. Eight standards of practice also specify the following:

1. Nondiscrimination: Counselors must avoid discrimination because of age, color, culture, disability, ethnic group, gender, race, religions, sexual orientation, marital status, or socioeconomic status (section A.2.a).
2. Disclosure to clients: Counselors must adequately inform clients, preferably in writing, regarding the counseling process and the counseling relationship at or before the time it begins and throughout the relationship (section A.3.a).
3. Dual relationships: Counselors must ensure that judgment is not impaired and that no exploitation occurs (section A. 6.a).
4. Sexual intimacies with clients: Counselors must not engage in any type of sexual intimacies with current clients (or) with former clients within a minimum of 2 years after terminating the counseling relationship (section A.6.b).
5. Group work: Counselors must protect clients during group work from physical or psychological trauma resulting from interactions during group work (section A.9.b).
6. Fees: Counselors must explain prior to entering the counseling relationship, financial arrangements related to professional services (section A. 10. A-d and A. 11.c).
7. Termination: Counselors must assist in making appropriate arrangements for the continuation of treatment of clients, when necessary, following termination of counseling relationships (section A. 11.a).
8. Inability to assist clients: Counselors must avoid entering or immediately terminate a counseling relationship if it is determined that they are unable to be of professional assistance to the client making an appropriate referral for the client (section A.11.b).

Confidentiality. Again the code is very clear about the client's right to privacy, stating, "Counselors respect their clients right to privacy and avoid illegal and unwarranted disclosures of confidential information ... (and) ... the right to privacy may be waived by the client or his or her legally recognized representative." Eight standards of practice specify particulars to guide and ensure client confidentiality:

1. Requirements: Counselors must keep information related to counseling services confidential unless disclosure is in the best interest of client, is required for the welfare of others, or is required by law when required, only information that is essential is revealed and the client is informed of such disclosures (section B.1.a+f).

2. Subordinates: Counselors must take measures to ensure that privacy and confidentiality of clients are maintained by subordinates (section B.1.h).
3. Group work: Counselors must clearly communicate to group members that confidentiality cannot be guaranteed in-group work (section B.2.a).
4. Family counseling: Counselors must not disclose information about one family member in counseling to another family member without prior consent (section B.2.b).
5. Records: Counselors must maintain appropriate confidentiality in creating, storing, accessing, transferring, and disposing of counseling records (section B.4.b).
6. Permission to record/observe: Counselors must obtain prior consent from clients in order to record electronically or observe sessions (section B.4.c).
7. Disclosure/transfer of records: Counselors must obtain client consent to disclose or transfer records to third parties, unless exceptions exist (section B.4.e).
8. Data disguise: Counselors must disguise the identity of the client when using data for training, research, or publication (section B.5.a).

Resolving Ethical Issues. The ACA Code is very clear that first and foremost it is the counselor's responsibility to be knowledgeable about the standards of resolving ethical issues. According to the Code, "Lack of knowledge or misunderstanding of an ethical responsibility is not a defense against a charge of unethical conduct" (section F.3.e). To resolve ethical issues, the *Standards of Practice* specify two very important aspects of ethical behavior:

1. Ethical behavior expected: Counselors must take appropriate action when they possess reasonable cause that raises doubts as to whether counselors or other mental health professionals are acting in an ethical manner (section H.2.a).
2. Cooperation with ethics committees: Counselors must cooperate with investigations, proceedings, and requirements of the ACA Ethics Committee or ethics committees of other duly constituted associations or boards having jurisdiction over those charged with a violation (section H.3).

NCDA National Ethical Standards and NBCC Code of Ethics

Just as the preamble for the ACA *Code of Ethics* states that the association is an educational, scientific, and professional organization whose members are dedicated to the enhancement of human development throughout the life span, NCDA *Ethical Standards* (revised 1991) adds, "the worth, dignity, potential, and uniqueness of each individual and thus, to the service of society." This additional emphasis on the "service of society," coupled with procedures for ethical complaints, are distinguishing factors in the two codes. Also, the ACA code includes an emphasis on teaching, training, and supervision, whereas NCDA offers separate sections on consulting and private practice. Because NBCC first adopted the NBCC *Ethical Standards* in 1987, today's NBCC *Code of Ethics*, amended October 31, 1997, parallels the same categories of the NCDA *Ethical Standards*. Also, the preamble:

> provides an expectation of and assurance for the ethical practice for all who use the professional services of an NBCC certificant. In addition, it serves the purpose of having an enforceable standard for all NBCC certificants and assures those served of some resources in case of a perceived ethical violation.

In addition, NBCC promotes counseling through certification and in pursuit of this mission the organization promotes:

- Quality assurance in counseling practice.
- The value of counseling.
- Public awareness of quality counseling practice.
- Professionalism in counseling.
- Leadership in credentialing.

Together these three associations guide counselors in their daily practice in face-to-face settings. A closer look at each of these documents includes guidelines for safeguarding services related to computers, which are addressed under the counseling relationship in Section A.12 a.–c. and under Section E. Evaluation, Assessment and Interpretation. NCDA also discusses appropriate ways to safeguard the client–counselor relationship under the Counseling Relationship, Section B., 16–17, under Measurement and Evaluation, Section C. Because the NBCC Code of Ethics was amended October 31, 1997, it specifically guides counselors in appropriate ways to safeguard the relationship, referring throughout the document to the NBCC standards for WebCounseling. In the same year, NCDA published *Guidelines for the use of the Internet for Provision of Career Information and Planning Services*, approved October 1997.

PRACTITIONER'S GUIDE TO ETHICAL DECISION MAKING

Searching for answers helped me clarify and resolve my own questions concerning safeguarding the client–counselor relationship. To guide me further, I followed the *Practitioner's Guide to Ethical Decision Making*, developed by Forester-Miller and Davis (1996). It is a model based on five moral principals, which bear repeating.

Autonomy

This principal addresses the concept of *independence*, allowing freedom of choice and action. It addresses the responsibility of the counselor to encourage clients to make their own decisions and to act on their own values. Two important considerations are addressed. The first is helping the client to understand how his or her values and actions may be received in the context of the society in which he or she lives and how these may impinge on the rights of others. The second relates to the client's ability to make competent choices, for example children and/or some individuals with mental handicaps should not be allowed to act on decisions that could harm the client or others.

Nonmaleficense

This concept means not causing harm to others. The principle is considered by some the most critical of all principles, often explained as "above all, do no harm." It reflects the idea of not inflicting intentional harm and not engaging in actions that risk harming others.

Beneficence

This principle reflects the counselor's responsibility to contribute the welfare of the client. It means doing good, being proactive, and also preventing harm when possible.

Justice

This principle does not mean treating all individuals the same. Forester-Miller and Davis cite Kitchener who stated that it means, "treating equals equally and unequals unequally but in proportion to their relevant differences" (p. 49). If an individual is to be treated differently, the counselor needs to be able to offer a rationale that explains the necessity and appropriateness of this action.

Fidelity

Fidelity includes the notions of loyalty, faithfulness, and honoring commitments. Clients must be able to trust the counselor and have faith in the therapeutic relationship if growth is to occur. Therefore, the counselor must take care not to threaten the therapeutic relationship nor leave obligations unfulfilled.

In addition to the five moral principles, the model offers a decision-making process. The model includes the following seven steps:

1. Identify the problem.
2. Apply the ACA Code of Ethics.
3. Determine the nature and dimensions of the dilemma.
4. Generate potential courses of action.
5. Consider the potential consequences of all options, choose a course of action.
6. Evaluate the selected course of action.
7. Implement the course of action.

Furthermore, the authors of the model noted that different professionals may implement different solutions or actions to the same situation. That is because there is rarely one right answer to a complex ethical dilemma. However, a systematic mode can assure the counselor will be able to give a professional explanation for the course chosen. Forester-Miller and Davis quoted Van Hoose and Paradise who suggested that a counselor is probably acting in an ethically responsible way concerning a client if:

1. He or she has maintained personal/professional honesty, coupled with
2. the best interests of the client,
3. without thought of malice or personal gain, and

4. can justify his or her actions as the best judgment of what should be done based upon the current state of the profession. (p. 58)

SUMMARY

The importance of listening to and honoring client voices cannot be over emphasized. Their numbers alone, more than 4,700 in one year to one counselor, demands attention. Their voices provide valuable insights as we define what is meant by online career counseling and the career counseling process. Client voices also support the observations of Lanning (cited in Morrissey, 1997), that is, to trust clients to choose what is best for them, a concept consistent with the ethical codes and standards for practice outlined by ACA, NCDA, and NBCC, the three professional organizations supporting our practice.

With few exceptions, I believe client voices tell us that safeguarding the online client–counselor relationship does not differ from in-person counseling situations. Consequently, I agree with Lanning when he asked:

> If a client is informed about the confidentiality risks of counseling (online or other) why do we think those clients cannot make intelligent informed choices about the Internet as we assume they do in traditional counseling? My office records can be stolen or broken into but we don't worry about that as much as security on the Internet. (p. 3)

If online clients are informed about confidentiality risks, who are we to think we know best about their needs? Who are we to think clients cannot make informed choices about what is best for them? And, I believe, trusting their judgment means honoring their choices. By including client voices in our discussions, our clients will contribute to the best practices in this new medium, including their visions about safeguarding this very special relationship.

In the next four chapters, I elaborate on how client voices help translate in-person career-counseling competencies for use in online settings. Chapter 4 introduces the importance of serving international and diverse populations, with the following three chapters focusing on counseling skills for a new context, including coaching for performance improvement, the role of online assessment, and providing appropriate information and referrals.

DISCUSSION QUESTIONS

1. Name the key points for online practice offered by the NBCC and the NCDA. Discuss differences. Which of these points are most relevant for your situation and practice? Why or why not?
2. Are client voices important to you, to your practice? Explain by providing an example from your practice.
3. Identify and discuss why clients find a career counselor's credentials important. Do you agree or disagree with the importance of credentials outlined in this chapter?
4. Which code of ethics or standard of practice is most helpful in guiding your practice?
5. Discuss Lanning's notion of paternalism. What does it mean to you? How does paternalism impact your practice?

PART

II

Translating Reflections Into Practice

Translating Reflections Into Practice is the organizing theme for the next four chapters. This section discusses competencies as well as issues posed by online career counseling clients. Chapter 4, Serving International Clients and Diverse Populations, offers responses for an international clientele, giving attention to issues not typically addressed in career counseling sessions, such as questions about immigration laws, work permits, visas, and international recruiters. Chapter 5, Coaching/Consulting for Performance Improvement, addresses the importance of defining the online skills, as well as differences in services offered by career counselors and career coaches. Chapter 6, Understanding the Use of Assessment Online, clarifies the link between career counseling and testing, demonstrating through client examples how online testing is implemented. The last chapter in this section, chapter 7, Providing Appropriate Information and Referrals, addresses the knowledge and resources considered essential in using technology to assist individuals with career planning. Links are provided for labor market information and related resources. Although logic suggests program promotion, management and implementation would be next, it is not emphasized in this section. Rather, this competency is integrated into the last three chapters, in Part III, Preparing for a Paradigm Shift.

4

Serving International Clients and Diverse Populations

In August 1998, when an overwhelming number of messages arrived at OCC.com for the Career Guru, I quickly noticed the complexity of the questions. Individual and cultural differences were obvious even among questions about resumes. Whether messages arrived from the states or foreign nationals, most provided personal details about individual circumstances. As I read each, I remember thinking, "I'm glad I'm not a novice. I would quit tomorrow." And, as each looked to this medium for hope, alternatives to their pain, I realized clients truly wanted interactive services with a qualified career counselor rather than strictly informational responses. As I struggled to conform to NCDA's concept of *career planning services*, I became more convinced that the NCDA definition needed expansion.

INTERNATIONAL CLIENTS

Just thinking about expanding the definition of online services gave me confidence. As overwhelmed as I felt from the surge of questions, I knew my confidence was grounded in years of practice and theory based on Rogerian concepts. My philosophy also was steeped in early experiences living and teaching in Southern California where acceptance and understanding for cultural differences and worldviews were part of daily life. More importantly, I drew strength from knowledge grounded in a code of professional ethics and standards of practice. I also knew my strength as a counselor lay in asking questions and seeking supervision when needed.

One in Ten Messages

Consequently when 1 out of 10 of the first 300 messages arrived from foreign nationals, it shouldn't have surprise me. Yet it did. Although I had served an international clientele, my clients never presented immigration issues. Without losing time, I learned immigration law and related resources. It was comforting to learn OCC.com already anticipated immigration questions posting a Web page for referral information. However, these resources did not fit all questions. To respond in a timely manner, I polished my online research skills by using browsers, search engines, and directories, toggling back and forth between these to identify appropriate sites. For some questions, my research efforts appeared effortless with instant searches producing just what was needed. Other efforts took 1 to 2 days. As I located sites for future reference, adding to my favorite places, these began to need their own organization to remain useful.

Parallels in Government Reports

Searching online kept me so busy that summer I hardly noticed newspaper reports on the rising numbers of immigrants in the United States. When I did note reports, I realized what I was observing online (1 in 10 messages on immigration issues) paralleled increases in immigrants coming from Asian and Hispanic countries. In an article by Randolph E. Schmid (1999), published by the Associated Press, the Census Bureau reported: "Overall, there were 25,208,000 foreign-born U.S. residents as of July 1, 1998—9.3 percent of the nation's population ... close to the 9.7 percent recorded in 1850." The article further noted that today's immigrants come from the South and Asia, a sharp contrast to the Europeans who flooded American shores in the 19th century. In my state of Indiana, the fastest growing segments of the population were reported as Asians and Hispanics.

Consistent with these reports are those published by the U.S. Department of Education (DOE) noting adult learners and nontraditional populations are a significant and diversifying force within the academic community. Accordingly, the DOE as cited by Rayman (1999), noting that "between 1991 and 1995, the number of Hispanic undergraduates increased by 26%, Asians increased by 24%, American Indians by 14% and Blacks by 9%" (p. 180).

Rayman (1999), writing about the importance of career services for the new millennium, called for the profession to design "new and alternative service delivery modes (e.g., bilingual counselors, counselors familiar with disability issues, services catering to returning adult students)." According to Rayman, "by redoubling our efforts to meet the changing career development needs of the increasingly diverse student body, we are likely to improve the quality of our services to everyone" (p. 180).

Although I found these reports on target and often comforting, I continued to journal about my feelings of surprise, noting and wishing I had more resources to offer clients whose stories, full of hope, expectation, or pain looked to this service for answers. With few exceptions, they wrote asking for the names of companies that wanted to hire foreign nationals. And, with fewer exceptions, asked the same question, "Please tell me which companies hired someone with my skills" or "Please send the name of recruiters who search for individuals with my background." Reflecting on messages and searching for answers related to immigration issues and diverse client populations led to my fifth lesson on the road.

LESSON 5: ONLINE CAREER COUNSELING BRIDGES CULTURAL DIFFERENCES

As noted in an earlier chapter, online career counseling services increase access and encourage clients to step forward with questions. In the case of international clients, the Internet provides clients increased access from remote areas and may serve as a strategy for bridging cultural differences.

Indications From the Literature

For instance, Sue and Sue (1990) pointed out the importance of understanding communication style differences, charting nonverbal and verbal styles for American Indians, Asian Americans/Hispanics, Whites and Blacks (see Table 4.1).

Notice there are five dimensions of differences among the groups in Table 4.1. The first dimension emphasizes differences in speech patterns, from speaking softly to speaking loudly to control the listener

Table 4.1
Communication Style Differences (Overt Activity Dimension–Nonverbal/Verbal)

American Indians	Asian/Hispanics	Whites	Blacks
1. Speak softly/ slower	1. Speak softly	1. Speak loud/to control listener	1. Speak with affect
2. Indirect gaze when listening or speaking	2. Avoidance of eye contact when listening or speaking to high-status persons	2. Greater eye contact when listening	2. Direct eye contact (prolonged) when speaking, but less when listening
3. Interject less seldom offer encouraging communication	3. Similar rules	3. head nods, nonverbal markers	3. Interrupt (turn-taking when can)
4. Delayed auditory (silence)	4. Mild delay	4. Quick responding	4. Quicker responding
5. Manner of expression low-keyed, indirect	5. Low-keyed, indirect	5. Objective, task-oriented	5. Affective, emotional interpersonal

and to speaking with affect. Eye contact is next, covering indirect gaze to avoidance when speaking to high-status persons, to greater eye contact when listening, and prolonged contact when speaking but listening less. The third and fourth dimensions range from interjecting less to head nods, to interrupting and taking turns, whereas the fourth dimension ranges from silence to delayed auditory to mild delay, to quick and quicker responses. The fifth dimension emphasizes manner, from low-keyed, indirect to objective task-oriented and affective emotional and interpersonal manner. Clearly, these five dimensions are important in face-to-face or in-person counseling sessions.

Style differences are less important with online career counseling or communicating through written text. There is no need to worry about misinterpreting or responding with bias based on how one speaks, let alone how one makes or does not make eye contact. The online process allows for all communication styles, thereby bridging cultural differences. This is equally true for the manner of communicating such as interjecting and/or responding with silence and emotion. And, for those international clients who value family input, who make decisions as a family unity, an online service provides the opportunity for whole-family participation. The family can gather around the computer to write questions and process responses before replying as a family unit.

Indications From Educational Attainment Levels and Client Anonymity

Messages from international clients also suggest these users are highly educated. Like online clients in the states, their messages reveal equal numbers with undergraduate, graduate, and professional degrees, indicating that a highly educated population uses this medium.

Furthermore, the medium's ability to provide anonymity increases the likelihood of bridging cultural differences, serving as a strategy to better serve international clients. For instance, unlike face-to-face counseling, online clients (e-mail career counseling clients) have the option of being completely anonymous, sharing whatever they like or want the counselor to know. These clients know they may ask a question without revealing their name, address, phone number, social security number, gender, sexual preference, even country, let alone worrying how their body language or nonverbal cues will be received. Knowing it will be harder for the counselor to speculate or judge particulars about their background, they need only write via e-mail. Yet, in the messages I received, complete anonymity was not a priority. Most volunteered their names, educational backgrounds, current employment, and their country of origin.

Perhaps a paradox occurs when there is the freedom to choose what will be shared. Freed to share or not share feelings, intimate details, and/or worry about misunderstandings arising from nonverbal communications, the client becomes more open. Perhaps this online medium allows clients to share information that according to Sue and Sue (1990), they would be reluctant to disclose in a face-to-face situation.

During the last weeks of August and the beginning of September 1998, no less than 30 foreign nationals wrote for employment information, with the majority mentioning their educational attainment (undergraduate and graduate degrees, with several in technical areas). The list speaks for itself, with each client beginning his or her message by stating, "I am ... "

- A civil engineer of Chinese origin based in Malaysia, with 18 years experience.

- An installation engineer, leading product, mostly working in southeast Asia, Korea, and Taiwan ... recently living in Thailand.
- A 1993 graduate in accounting and economics from a Canadian university.
- An SCADA/PLC project engineer presently working in Muscat (Oman).
- A civil engineer living in Pakistan.
- A Malaysian, seeking an IT position in the UK or USA.
- An Indonesian, working on a visa so I can migrate and live in the USA with my fiancée.
- In Namibia, everyday is painful for me.
- A civil engineer for 17 years working in the Middle East.
- An MBA currently completing my education in Lausanne.
- A director of human resources for an international company in Canada.
- An executive office assistant in Dubai for a five-star hotel.
- A perplexed in Calgary, Alberta Canada.
- A Canadian seeking employment in the USA.
- A leading system integrator in India.
- An engineering graduate in the field of telecommunications from Bangalore, India.
- Currently working in Singapore as a consultant (analyst/programmer) for a bank.
- In the Ukraine and want to find a job in an English speaking country.
- A B.E. in mechanical engineering from Mysore University, Mysore graduate.
- An accounting technician from the UK.
- An IT consultant, employed in Thailand and looking for work in USA.
- Currently living in Switzerland, and want to work in London.
- An industrial relations specialist from India.
- An MBA from UTS, Syndney, Australia.
- From Malta, 22 years old.
- An Indian national residing in Bahrain.
- A medical doctor (MD), 44 years old, in Buenos Aires.
- A young man living in Ghana.
- A singer (base) from Moscow.
- A Korean with work experience in the U.S. and Canada, willing to pay moving expenses.

Clearly, the list represents an educated population, one sophisticated enough to know the risks of posting privileged information online. Yet, anxious for answers to their career dilemmas or to realize their goals, they step forward, seeking answers to their individual circumstances. Although their circumstances differed, the most common questions were the following two: "Please tell me which companies hire someone with my skills" and "Please send the names of recruiters who search for individuals with my background." To their replies, I often began by recognizing their plight, stating something like: "More than anything, I wish there were recruiters to help. Unfortunately, to be employed in the USA, the law requires you either have an established residency or possess a work visa." Then I would address their individual concerns and/or refer them to immigration links on the OCC.com Web pages. Or, if I suspected they were new to the site and might have difficulty navigating its links, I would cut and paste the actual quotations or references.

Department of State Resources

The following is a quote I often included within my replies.

> According to the U.S. Department of State, exceptions exist for persons in shortage occupations and those demonstrating "exceptional ability" in business, science, or arts, as defined by the State Department. Currently, the law allots 140,000 employment-based visas within five categories:
> 1. Priority workers (40,000), people who have "extraordinary ability" or who are "outstanding professors and researchers" or "certain Multinational executives and managers";
> 2. 40,000 (plus any left over from the first) go to "members of the professions holding advanced degrees or aliens of exceptional ability";
> 3. 40,000 visas are issued to skilled workers, professionals, and other workers;
> 4. Up to 10,000 are issued to special immigrants, including ministers, religious workers, and others;
> 5. Up to 10,000 are issued to persons who have between $500,000 and $3 million to invest in a job-creating enterprise in the USA. In this case, at least 10 USA workers must be employed by each investor.

Following this type of quote, whenever possible, I include information aimed at the client's unique circumstance and/or alternative ways to enter the country. I also provide links to the resources cited and/or offer additional resources for follow-up. For example, I point out information related to:

1. Employers. Before visas can be issued in the second and third prefer-ence categories, employers must first obtain a "labor certification" from the U.S. Department of Labor confirming that there are not suffi-cient U.S. workers who are able, qualified, and willing to perform the work ... and ... that employment of the alien will not adversely affect the wages and working conditions of U.S. workers.

2. Diversity Visas. In addition to the preference system, there is one other way ... it is called a Diversity Visa, an annual lottery program to encour-age immigration from countries that send few immigrants ... like France. In this category, 55,000 visas are randomly awarded by the U.S. State Department. If lucky enough to win a Diversity Visa, the per-son is permitted to reside permanently in the U.S. solely on the basis of his or her native country's designation by the U.S. State Department.

3. Additional Resources. You may read more about this and the prefer-ence system at: http://www.immigrationforum.org. If you cannot reach the site directly, link there through the American Immigration Lawyers Association at: http://www.aila.org. Good luck and I hope this helps.

INFLUENCING SKILLS

According to Sue and Sue (1990), to avoid "placing Asian Americans in the uncomfortable and oppressed position," counselors should utilize influencing versus attending skills, that is, they should provide clients with the advice and information they seek rather than rely on reflection of feelings. Sue and Sue (1990) cited a study by Atkinson, Maruyama, and Matsui, in which the findings showed that "counselors who use the directive approach were rated more credible and approachable than those using the nondirective counseling approach" (p. 69).

International Students Versus Established Professionals

In contrast to the large numbers of established professionals using online career counseling services, fewer international students ac-cessed the services. Perhaps their universities already offered the ca-reer services they sought or perhaps aspirations for higher education assured these students its own type of career development. In any event, fewer international student sent messages. When they did, I re-sponded to them in ways similar to their counterparts in the profes-sions, that is, I provided immigration information. And, often I added information similar to resources offered to U.S. students, that is, the importance of conducting career research, enrolling in internships, and networking with professors. The following is a message from one female student:

I am a student who is doing her graduation in Political Science (IInd year, we have III years in graduation B.A (Hons)). Simultaneously I am pursuing a Computer Course from NIIT (National Institute Information Technology). I am doing a 3 year course where I would be learning programming in Internet, Visual Basic etc. At the moment I am doing Sybase and by December I shall finish One year in NIIT. In this one year I shall also finish C& C++. However I have quite some knowledge in software's like MS-Word, MS-Excel, Access, Internet(how to form Web Pages, this does not include Java), Quality Management(we have Seminars etc where we are marked on the basis of our Presentation in class), LAN, Application Development etc. At the moment I am busy with my studies but I wish and pray to get a good job in New York or Chicago(USA). I shall be obliged if you could help me by suggesting as to what I should do in the mere future and what kind of job should I pursue. Please send the mail to any of the following ... Thanking you

Notice her use of language. She writes: "I wish and pray to get a good job in New York or Chicago (USA)" and she is seeking suggestions. Notice, in my response, I avoid direct advice. Instead I offer several suggestions and alternatives for her to choose from:

There are several things to do to prepare for a job in the USA:
1. American Embassy or Consulate. Write or visit the American Embassy or Consulate stationed in your country. There you can gather information on immigration laws and companies doing business with and in the U.S. You may also learn about companies seeking employees with your skills. If that is not convenient, use links on our site to make a visit.
2. Immigration laws. Learn all you can about the immigration laws and restrictions which may apply to you. Link on our site to the Career Resources page. At the Career Resources page, click on Relocation, then Immigration.
3. Job options. Read various job descriptions on our site to identify positions which appeal to you. You can search by city, by state, or search by job area such as IT, etc.
4. Network. While you are still studying in your country, network there, that is, discuss your situation with your professors, professionals you know and trust as well as those you admire. Or, become involved with professional groups on and off campus. Attend international conferences whenever you can. These are excellent opportunities to showcase your skills through presentations and/or by networking with prospective contacts and employers worldwide.

5. Internships. Ask your professors about internships that may be available in your field. An internship can provide valuable experience and make you more marketable for positions in this country.

6. Post your resume. Remember to post your resume on our site. Good Luck. Sincerely, The Career Guru

Although OCC.com had excellent online resources for foreign nations to access, and despite efforts to educate myself on immigration issues, I still felt inadequate as I responded to the needs of international clients. To feel more comfortable I contacted three local resources. These resources included the Indiana University Law School, the International Center of Indianapolis, and Senator Lugar's Office. At all three locations I spoke with immigration specialists. What I discovered was what I already knew. There are no lists of employers or recruiters seeking foreign nationals. Instead, all three offices recommended immigration attorneys who could be contacted through the Immigration Lawyers Association at http://www.aila.org, an affiliated organization of the American Bar Association. Or, they recommended resources provided through embassies many of which offered resource centers and assistance at http://www.embassy.org. There are no lists because immigration for employment in the United States requires eligibility and sponsorship. Without sponsorship, immigration can be very difficult. With sponsorship from a U.S. corporation, the process is simplified.

Example From Practice

Interestingly, too, the director of the International Center believes corporate American is not the only path to sponsorship. She discussed multiple ways for making contacts and gaining sponsorship, many of which are similar strategies to what career counselors tell any job hunter. These strategies include having a career focus, developing a plan, and networking with everyone you know. She said she suggests individuals network in their country with church groups and/or professional associations, or work closely with contacts at their embassy. In other words, just as U.S. clients need to be aware of the hidden job market, international clients also need to be aware of this strategy. So often they depend or look to the advertised job market, becoming discouraged when their applications do not result in offers. Accessing the hidden market through networking may be the immigration client's most important skill. And, serving an international market may very well mean that career counselors need to emphasize the importance of networking, pointing out how many opportunities may be missed without it. In turn, counselors may need to teach and coach clients on the art of networking.

Networking is a Critical Skill for International Clients. Although networking is a job search strategy I often recommend, it took me a year, plus direct contact with international clients in my private practice, to learn how critical this skill can be for international clients. Here's what made it so real.

Exactly 1 year after starting online work, I received a call from Career Resources in Cleveland, Ohio, asking me if I was available to provide Destination Services for one of their clients who was coming to Indianapolis from the British Isles. Destination Services are new services offered by an employer to an employee who accepts a position in the states. Once the client accepts the position, a counselor is contracted to meet the client/family at their destination point. Generally, the destination point is the airport, where the counselor meets the arriving plane and assists the client/family as they acclimate to their new community. Up to 40 hours of assistance is generally provided, which is customized to meet the individual needs of the client or family. In the case of my clients, the service began by assisting them with their rental car, temporary housing, and registration at the local social security office. It also included tours to learn the city and to identify appropriate housing, places of worship, leisure time activities, and shopping malls. In some cases, the client might choose assistance for the spouse and children, such as information on day care, private schools, and/or special needs, including information for spouses interested in volunteer activities or returning to school. In addition to learning about the city and the options it offered, my client and his wife wanted to do some comparison shopping for prices of food, clothing, and household furnishings. We also included a trip to a car dealership to compare new and used car prices.

Client's Networking Story

On one of our trips I asked, "By the way, how did you land your job here?" To my surprise, the client said it happened through networking.

The client said he always wanted to come to the United States. Before he proposed, he even told his bride "eventually I'll be working in the States." Although he had no real plan, he knew this was one of his goals. As a mechanical engineer, he held a responsible job abroad. He often spoke with many suppliers around the world, one of which was located in Indianapolis, Indiana. As he described it, one day he called the Indianapolis supplier, asking to speak with his counterpart (another mechanical engineer). To his surprise he was told, there wasn't anyone in that position. The position was actually vacant. Discovering this, he asked a few more questions and in reply heard, "If you're interested in the position, fax us your resume." And, as the saying goes, the rest is history. He faxed his resume, received a phone call, and was interviewed via satellite video. When he was offered the job, he accepted. The whole process took less than 6 weeks.

National Providers/Associations Concur

What my client described not only serves as a lesson in networking, it is a model for job hunting internationally. It is also a model of how job hunting strategies are changing, or what Stephanie Armour (1999) proposed in her article focusing on "the new interview etiquette." According to the article, the rules are changing fast: "Now technology and a tight labor market are ushering in an age of virtual interviews, legal contracts, psychological testing and hiring by committee. Offers are made faster; interviews are short and intense" (p. 1).

Resource Careers, Cleveland, Ohio. Given these changes, the importance of networking and providing appropriate services for international clients cannot be emphasized enough. Sponsorship is expensive for employers and they want it to work, suggesting that the right fit is very important. An e-mail I received in the summer of 1999, from Mindy Bartholomae, manager of International Relocation Programs, Resources Careers, Cleveland, Ohio, illustrates my point:

Hello To All!!

I just spent 4 days in New Orleans at the Employee Relocation Council's International Symposium on International Assignment Management. Wow, was it ever energizing and so affirming of this service that we offer to foreign nationals coming to work in the U.S.!

Fortunately, an awareness of the need for destination services is growing amongst corporate HR departments and the demand will increase astronomically. So many companies are "going global"! (With) An average of 1 million dollars per 2–3 year assignment!!! It certainly behooves the company to make it all work!!

Because the service we provide is so very personalized, our goal is to present ourselves in a similar light. I know you all have "gone the extra mile" with the clients you've served. And it really means allot. Thanks so much for your support.
Mindy Bartholomae

Professional Association Example.   Professional associations are another excellent example of how foreign nationals can begin to network and increase their potential not only for immigration contacts and opportunities, but for career development once they are here. Not all international clients write about immigration issues. Many already in this country write for assistance with on-the-job situations or issues of discrimination. For instance, for international clients who are from Asia, I often make referrals to the Naitonal Association of Asian American Professionals at http://www.naaap.org. NAAAP is a nonprofit 501(C) (3), all-volunteer organization. Their mission is to promote the personal and professional development of the Asian American community. Clearly, networking is among the goals of this organization. As stated on their Web site:

Our membership comprises a diverse group of individuals with various levels of education and work experience. By pooling resources to support common goals, we strive not only to benefit our members, but more importantly, the entire Asian American community and our society at large. NAAAP is involved in many joint projects with Asian American community service groups, professional organizations and university student groups. As a result, our members are exposed to a broad yet focused range of activities and are given the opportunity to meet and work wit other Asian American community leaders. To accomplish our goals we:
a. Sponsor and support activities that enhance the cultural awareness and perception of Asian Americans;
b. Provide resources and assistance to the Asian American community and Asian American university students;
c. Promote Pan-Asian unity through fellowship and professional networking;
d. Enhance the business and career environment for Asian Americans.

Example From Online Practice.   Here is an example of an international client, already in the states, requesting advice. His question asks about pay equity and recognition on the job. Notice how he begins his question with an apology, writing:

Dear Career Guru:
This question may be politically improper to ask. I am an Asian American.
I often feel like the company or employer treats me unfairly in terms of
pay and recognition. Do you have any suggestions or ideas on how to
break the barrier to gain acceptance and trust at work?

As a counselor, I believe it is part of my job to help clients normalize their feelings, what some call *reframing client messages*. I do this by both reflecting their feelings or restating what they write in positive terms, and providing them appropriate information for their review. As evidenced by client responses, I believe this is not inconsistent with the earlier suggestions offered by Sue and Sue (1990) regarding preferred counselor behaviors. Also, evidenced by client responses, I believe instruction and/or teaching is part of the online career counseling process. My reply to this client was:

Any question applying to a great many people is not politically improper, particularly the two issues you present.

1. Employment discrimination. Even with laws against employment discrimination, discrimination can and does continue to happen. However, regarding pay equity, the law is on your side, meaning you may be able to negotiate for a pay increase. Ideally, you would do this when you receive an employment offer. If you didn't negotiate then, the time to renegotiate your salary is at your annual review, when you discuss with your supervisor your contributions and value to the company. By learning about industry salary standards for you field, as well as in your location and company, you can prepare to present your case. To read more about salary surveys link at http://www.occ.com/occ/career/salary

2. Gaining recognition. Gaining trust and acceptance leading to recognition is a more complex issue than pay equity. No laws govern recognition. Recognition, acceptance, and trust also mean different things to different people. Sometimes cultural differences keep us apart or separate us unnecessarily. You already may have your employer's acceptance and trust yet not recognize it. For example, many White males use joking, teasing, and/or humor to pay compliments to each other, believing the other accepts this behavior as a sign of admiration or respect. Sometimes, too, they use this method of communication to correct one another, as a way to say, "shape up!" Communicating with humor can be very confusing. Here are two suggestions to determine if this is what's happening in your case:

   a. Read more about communication styles, particularly cross-cultural styles. There are several books on the subject which you may identify by searching at http://www.amazon.com

b. Gain support from like-minded people. In your case, I'd suggest contacting one of the chapters of the National Association for Asian American Professionals (NAAAP). Among the goals of NAAAP are to promote professional networking and to enhance the business and career environment of Asian American Professionals. Link there at: http://www.naaap.org. Belonging to NAAAP or a similar organization is a good strategy for breaking down barriers as well as enhancing your long-term career development goals. Good luck, and I hope this helps.

His return message was brief yet speaks for itself. He replies:

Thank you for responding to my message. Your input has given me insight on how I should handle the issue and myself. You are a true help. Thank you.

SUMMARY

Ten percent of the messages from an international clientele suggests we need online career counseling services offering resources for a global marketplace. Government reports indicate the largest increases in immigration are the Hispanic and Asian populations, with evidence suggested by a proportionate rise in these populations on college campuses. To meet new demands for career services in the millennium, Raymon (1999) called for "redoubling our efforts to meet the changing career development needs of the increasingly diverse student body" (and noted) "we are likely to improve the quality of our services to everyone" (p. 180).

I concur with Raymon, believing improvement in one area benefits all. Online career services may be one strategy that would redouble our efforts, particularly for an educated population who are most likely to utilize online career services. Further messages from an educated population suggest individualized career information is more important than confidentiality issues. This is evidenced in messages volunteering personal details regarding individual differences and situations. To reach their goals, online clients appear willing to waive their rights to privacy over the Internet.

More than any other client population's messages, international messages convince me of the need to expand the definition of online career planning services as defined by NCDA. Without some type of interaction between the client and the counselor, NCDA's definition of *career planning services* becomes incomplete. It describes services similar to an electronic book or message board rather than a dynamic relationship created through text or an interactive service between clients and qualified career counselors.

DISCUSSION QUESTIONS

1. Characterize international clients who utilize online career counseling services.
2. Discuss the advantages and disadvantages of using online career counseling with international populations. Give examples.
3. What are the most effective counselor skills suggested by Sue and Sue (1990)? Do you agree or disagree with this perspective? Why or why not?
4. Do you agree that networking is a critical skill for international clients to develop? Why or why not? Give an example to support your position.
5. Do you agree with the notion that online career counseling services bridge cultural differences? Provide evidence to support your response.

5

Coaching/Consulting for Performance Improvement

Like the importance of networking as a career search strategy, coaching/consulting for performance improvement, is an important counselor skill for e-mail counseling. Coaching is not only what Sue and Sue (1990) cited in studies as increasing credibility for counselors who work with international clients, it is listed among the 11 Career Counseling Competencies published by the NCDA in the revised version, 1997. Listed sixth, coaching, consultation, and performance improvements, is a critical skill dealing with a complexity of client issues related to job performance, training, advancement, and addressing issues beyond career choice.

WORKFORCE DYNAMICS CREATE NEW INTERVENTIONS

Traditionally, in the early and middle decades of the 20th century, career counseling theory focused on career choice and career decision-making models, rather than issues of performance, advancement, and leadership development, with earlier models implemented through school or university settings, and/or rehabilitation centers like services offered to disabled veterans.

The 1960s and 1970s

In the late 1960s and continuing through the 1970s, the rise of minorities and women on college campuses and in the workforce, gave way to new services and career development models more relevant to the issues raised in the civil rights movement and by the feminist agenda. Women and minorities in this country sought career development beyond the issue of choice and decision making. Many sought advancement opportunities as well as leadership, creating new models, that laid the groundwork for today's strategies, including online services offered to a global audience.

The 1980s

Massive layoffs in the auto industry and later in defense plants during the 1980s also contributed to the rise of new services and models. Starting in the early 1980s, the country became aware of the devastating effects that unemployment created in families and communities, dubbing many cities in the midwest, The Rust Belt. As the 1980s progressed and plant closings spread to defense plants as well as the garment industry, many factories continued to close, this time moving abroad. The need for services intensified, resulting in the rise of legislation as a remedy. For example, laws were passed to ensure workers received advanced notification, with many plants required to provide a minimum of 60 days notice. Legislation also led to the development of job training programs to create new employment options for the displaced. These programs now fall under the umbrella of nationwide workforce development offices. Today, many states offer government-sponsored career centers. Originally, designed to serve the needs of laid-off workers, these centers, popularly known as one-stop career centers, offer individual counseling, vocational testing, job training, and placement services as well as a national data bank of job positions.

The 1990s

No longer limited to displaced workers, one-stop centers in the 1990s served factory workers as often as entry-level managers and professionals through the senior ranks. The centers offered many displaced employees, mid-level and senior managers training programs in technology to develop proficiency in computer skills neglected earlier in their careers. This change or expansion of service to mid-level and senior managers was the direct result of continuing changes throughout the 1990s dubbed by many as the decade of acquisitions and mergers.

With scores of corporations reorganizing, relocating, slimming down, right-sizing, and/or downsizing, a new population of middle managers experienced a rising need for services to match their circumstances.

NCDA GUIDELINES ON COACHING AND CONSULTATION SKILLS

These vast changes reflected in legislation and the delivery of services did not happen by accident. The expansion is the direct result of counselors in the field applying their coaching and consulting skills with key decision makers within communities and government agencies. The NCDA's (1997a) publication, *Career Counseling Competencies, Revised Version, 1997*, articulates a broad scope for coaching skills, including the ability to do the following:

1. Use consultation theories, strategies, and models.
2. Establish and maintain a productive consultative relationship with people who can influence a client's career.
3. Help the general public and legislators understand the importance of career counseling, career development, and life–work planning.
4. Impact public policy as it relates to career development and workforce planning.
5. Analyze future organizational needs and current level of employee skills and develop performance improvement training.
6. Mentor and coach employees.

Coaching, consultation, and performance improvement, clearly demonstrates that the field of career counseling is not only about the enhancement of the "worth, dignity, potential and uniqueness of each individual," its mission is dedicated to the "service of society," or consultation that enhances the resources of the wider community, our society. Coaching, usually associated with mentoring and advising activities, is but one aspect of this comprehensive skills set.

Consequently, today, growing numbers of men as well as women ask complex questions and expect answers. They inquire not only about complex situations related to working from home, telecommuting, and/or juggling multiple jobs and roles, they ask about discrimination law, including issues related to ageism. They also ask how to avoid downsizing; survive company takeovers, multiple downsizing experiences; and/or improve performance by dealing with difficult bosses and relationships with others, whether co-workers or family members.

One might think these changes would demand and give rise to an increasing number of certified career counselors to address these complex issues. Yet, over the last decade, there has been a decline in these ranks. Instead, there has been a rise in the number of paraprofessionals to meet the demand. Paraprofessionals not only serve diverse populations through government one-stop centers, they have swelled the ranks of outplacement professionals and given rise to what is known as a new breed of helpers, career coaches.

ONLINE CAREER COACHING VERSUS CAREER COUNSELING

The term *career coach* is not to be confused with the term as it is applied to NCCCs. Although the two share some similarities, the groups are not the same. Their mission, aims, training, codes of ethics and standards of practice differ in several ways. As Shannon Anderson (personal communication, 1999), an NCCC and director of career services at the extension office on the campus of the University of California at San Diego, recently noted: "Career counselors can provide not only coaching skills, they can provide assessment and individual counseling for their clients. The career coach is limited to offering only one skills set. So often clients present issues which demand a professional who provides more."

Responsible coaches recognize their limitations. Cheryl Richardson (Campbell, 1999), past president of the International Coach Federation (ICF), is quoted as saying, "Coaching is really about taking action." She further noted that in the early 1990s when coaching was in its infancy, it attracted only high-salaried executives who were looking for ways to boost their careers. According to Richardson, the popularity of coaches grew because "Unlike a therapist, a coach helped them look to the future instead of the past and to actions instead of causes" (p. 1).

In the same article, Campbell referred to observations by Bobette Reeder, vice president of member development for ICF. Ms. Reeder attributed the growth of coaches to technology and new awareness about options, stating: "people feel increasingly isolated because so many are working by themselves, whether it's at home or in a room with 100 cubicles. It's more difficult for workers to develop relationships with someone who can coach them as a mentor or friend" (p. 2). Other coaches in the field see their role as helping clients find answers inside themselves, with the coach there to hold them accountable for taking action when they say they will.

Career Coaching Standards

In many ways, the rise of career coaches parallels the rise of commercial online career centers. Seeking to assist job seekers, these centers hire coaches to answer online questions from users, offering a public forum to help users access resources for action. The ICF site is one such example. It can be visited at http://www.coachfederation.org. On this site the ICF definition of coaching is posted as:

> The International Coach Federation adheres to a form of coaching that honors the client as the expert in his/her personal and/or professional life and believes that every client is creative, resourceful, and whole. Standing on this foundation, the coach's responsibility is to:
> 1. Discover, clarify, and align with what the client wants to achieve.
> 2. Encourage client self-discovery.
> 3. Elicit client-generated solutions and strategies.
> 4. Hold the client as responsible and accountable.

The ICF lists an additional 18 standards of conduct, calling on coaches to treat "all clients with dignity as free and equal human beings." The standards also call on coaches to identify their level of competence and "not misrepresent my qualifications, expertise, or experience as a professional coach." Coaches are to clarify the terms of the coaching relationship, recommending different coaches and/or resources when appropriate. In addition, coaches are expected to share their "skills and practices with other interested coaches," to give "full acknowledgment to the work and contributions of others," and to "respect copyrights, trademarks and intellectual property rights and comply with laws and my agreements concerning these rights." A complete list of the 18 standards can be reviewed at http://www.coachfederation.org.

Career Coaching Disclaimers

In December 1999, Interim Services, Inc., now Spherion Corporation, launched an interactive career resource web site, called CareerZone at http://www.careerzone.com. Here, visitors can accept the services of career coaches. In contrast to the ICF organizational example of coaching, the Interim site provides a picture of career coaching in practice. For example, on the "CareerZone, Ask the Expert Page," there is a clear disclaimer for the user to read and learn what questions are and are not appropriate to ask of experts. It begins with an introduction about the career coaches, followed by a list of disclaimers:

CareerZone.com Ask the Expert Disclaimer.

The Career Coaches who respond to your question are experts in the field of career management. However, we want you to understand that there are limitations on the assistance that can be provided to you. The following disclaimers apply to this feature.

1. CareerZone.com has a policy of providing coaching services only to adults age 18 or over. If a Career Coach receives any indication that the person they are communicating with is a minor they will cease providing advice.

2. The Career Coach will not provide legal advice. Examples of questions where legal advice is being sought and therefore will not be answered are:

    a. Am I entitled to unemployment compensation (or workers' compensation, disability pay, etc.) from my employer (or former employer)?

    b. Doesn't my former employer have to provide me with severance pay (vacation pay, bonus payments, other payments)?

    c. What are my rights under the EEO (wage hour, FMLA, ADA, etc.) laws?

    d. To what extent can an employer consider my criminal (credit) record in its dealing with me?

3. The Career Coach will provide assistance to you in the form of options for you to consider. Career Coaches have been advised not to direct you to the specific course of action to take. The ultimate responsibility for your actions remains with you. Examples of this might include:

    a. Do you think I should confront my boss about my problems with co-workers (or other work issues)?

    b. Would you advise me to demand (or ask for) a raise?

    c. I have applied for a job that I think is perfect for me. The employer I applied with is acting very slowly in filling the position. How much contact should I have with the hiring manager so the employer will know I am interested and keep me in mind for the job?

Interim Services Inc. does not accept any liability for the advice given by a career coach.

A careful review of the disclaimers provided by Interim Services, Inc., on its CareerZone.com page, specifically demonstrate what is appropriate for online questions and responses regarding client roles and responsibilities as well as the content of their questions, plus a clear outline of the roles and responsibilities of the career coach. For example, the statements are very clear that only services will be provided to those over the age of 18. Furthermore, it is clear that questions about employee rights, those that are legal in nature, will not be answered in this format.

On the Monster.com site, where public message boards post client questions and responses from career coaches and the general public, the Monster.com guidelines for posting add another dimension to disclaimers.

Monster.com Message Board Guidelines.

The Message Boards were established to allow visitors an opportunity to share ideas, questions and comments with each other regarding the job search process and other career related topics. Please note that we reserve the right to remove any messages that are determined inappropriate or off-topic. If you have any further questions, please refer to Monster.com's Terms of Use at http://www.monster.com/terms/. If you read any posts in violation of the following, please e-mail the post URL and subject to: community@monster.com. By posting on any of Monster.com's message boards, you agree not to post:

1. Material that is copyrighted or trademarked
2. Material that reveals trade secrets
3. Material that infringes on any other intellectual, privacy or publicity rights of others
4. Material that is obscene, defamatory, threatening, harassing, abusive, hateful or embarrassing to another person or entity
5. Sexually explicit images or statements
6. Advertisements or solicitations of business, chain letters or pyramid schemes
7. Material that is intended to damage or interfere with any system, data or information
8. Material in violation of any applicable law or regulation
9. Any incomplete, false or inaccurate biographical information (i.e., you are not permitted to impersonate another person)

LESSON 7: BOUNDARY SETTING FOR ONLINE COUNSELING EFFECTIVENESS

These disclaimers and message board guidelines from career coaches and online career centers offer career counselors additional and specific guidelines or boundaries related to the online medium, particularly when the medium is a public forum versus a one-one-one experience through e-mail career counseling. The guidelines neither detract from career counseling standards nor conflict our codes of ethics. Rather, career counselors may have something to learn from online coaches about boundary setting in this medium.

Reflecting on the importance of boundary setting reminds me of a saying purported by one of the leaders in the marriage and family counseling field, I believe it was Whitaker who stated that as counselors, "we need to win the battle for structure and loose the battle for power." By this he meant, it is our role to define the parameters of the counseling session, that is, it is our role, our job to determine when and where the sessions will be held, the duration, fees, and areas of expertise or practice we will address with clients. Once this is established and the client agrees to the structure of the counseling, it becomes our job to then lose the battle for power. The battle for power refers to the client's readiness and willingness to change, to move forward, or to decide on whether or not to take action. Whitaker believed the client must have this freedom to choose in order for trust in the counselor to occur, and change in the client to transpire. The battle for power (defining client issues and outcomes) is one of the major differences between career coaching as a specialty and career counseling.

Differences Between Career Coaching and Career Counseling

It is important to make distinctions between online career coaching and career counseling. First, career coaching is offered online as a public forum. This means it is a service wherein clients submit questions that are publicly posted online to be answered by career experts who take turns responding to posted messages, generally within 48 to 72 hours. In a coaching situation, the goal is to provide information for the client to take action, and have someone to whom they can be accountable for follow-up. In contrast, online career counseling is similar to telephone counseling in that is it is offered on a one-to-one basis and "implies a deeper level of involvement with the client." Online career counseling is confined to: e-mail career counseling practiced on an individualized, one-to-one basis, with the e-mail messages and responses written between the client and the career counselor within a specified time frame, similar to individual appointments.

A deeper level of involvement with the client is what Whitaker meant by losing the battle for power or trusting the client. In this case, transformation rests not in action alone, insight may be its own reward, as are feelings of affirmation and self-worth. A tangible outcome is not necessary to measure the counseling process as successful. Nonetheless, I believe the boundary guidelines developed and established by career coaches are valuable additions for career counselor to incorporate in their practices.

Example 1 From an Online Career Coach

Here is an example of how a career coach might answer one of the common question presented by clients online. The question is: "Should I leave my current company because the job is no longer a challenge?" Following is the response:

> I am not in the position to answer your question; only you can determine what is best for you. Before you answer this question, however, you might want to carefully weigh the pros and cons of staying where you are against finding another job. Ask your self what is of top priority to you at this time in your career. How does leaving to go to another company fit with your overall career plan? Are the working environment, pay and positive co-worker relationships enough of an incentive to stay where you are? Is there a guarantee that these will be as positive with another company? If not, are you willing to loose these positive aspects? Is there any way you can persuade your supervisor to add additional duties that might be more interesting to your current job description or move you into another department where the job might be more challenging? If so, would you be more content with the current company? After you have answered these and similar questions you will be better able to make a decision that best fits your current needs and long term career goals. Thanks for your question and best of success in your future endeavors. Best regards, Career Coach

Example 2 From an Online Career Coach

Many clients ask questions about the interview process. They want to know what to expect, what questions they will be asked or how to handle a difficult question. One of the most common interview questions asked by online clients appears here with suggested responses from career coaches:

Why did you leave your last employer?

In his book, "Knock Um Dead," Martin Yate suggests six reasons for leaving a position:
- Challenge: You weren't able to grow professionally in that position.
- Location: The commute was unreasonably long.
- Advancement: There was nowhere for you to go. You had the talent, but there were too many people ahead of you.
- Money: You were underpaid for your skills and contribution.
- Pride or prestige: You wanted to be with a better company.
- Security: The company was not stable.

Notice these examples from online coaches are different from the career counseling messages offered in earlier chapters where attention is paid to the tone of the message, the client's choice of language, and attention to affect. Responding to tone, language, and/or the context of a person's life are counseling skills that also include affirming or normalizing client feelings with attention to client attitudes and deci-sion-making processes. Career counselors know the importance of attending skills even when answering commonly asked questions like those previously. For example, one of the most commonly asked ques-tions by both men and women relates to working at home. Here is a question from a woman, holding a part-time job that she would like to turn into a part-time telecommuting position once she starts her fam-ily. She writes:

> When is the best time to tell my boss I'd like to telecommute once I have children? I have a half-time job that would work well as a telecommut-ing position. My husband and I would like to start a family in the next year and have thought about my setting up at home to be with the baby. How should I approach my employer about this? Should I wait until I am pregnant and then lay out a proposal for working from home, or should I talk with my employer about this idea before I get pregnant?

Notice she is not pregnant, rather she wants to be. She also wants to make plans to negotiate with her employer about a part-time arrange-ment, asking when is the best time to tell him. Her question is written in a matter-of-fact style, indicating she is not suffering from undue anx-iety or excessive exhilaration, both emotions that often prevent a client from listening to counselor suggestions or accessing resources. Be-cause women still have fewer workplace mentors than men, and in many cases none at all, I respond to her as I would a client or student I might be mentoring, pointing out certain workforce realities.

> Naturally, you know your employer best. However, since you are in a part-time position, I would wait to discuss any negotiation until you're actually pregnant with dates, etc. Why? Anything can happen between now and then. If, for example, your employer is looking to cut costs and you've already declared you'd like to work from home this could be a ra-tionale to cut your job before you've a chance at telecommuting. Also, as hard as it might be, I wouldn't recommend sharing your plans to start a family either. Some employers, even the most supportive ones, will hear that and begin planning your replacement. I've seen stranger things happen and when they do, the easy way out for the employer is to say, "remember when you told us ..." By waiting, you'll be buying time to plan your proposal. To do this, check out the policies stated in your employee handbook. You may find the best way to approach your employer is by quoting policy on flexible arrangements, job sharing, and

telecommuting. And, while you are preparing your proposal you may find the following sites helpful: Home-Based Working Moms—a national association for work at home mothers at http://www.hbwm.com or the online magazine for work at home moms at http://www.wahm.com. Also, New Ways to Work (NWW) in San Francisco has been advocating for flexible arrangements for moms for over 20 years. The NWW site currently offers a list of resources on telecommuting at http://www.nww.org. The International Telework Association and Council is another good site at http://www.telecommute.org/ as are the telecommuting resources listed with the Society for Human Resource Management at http://www.shrm.org/hrlinks/flex.htm. This may be more information than you requested yet may be important in preparing your proposal. And if you want a second opinion on timing and negotiations, check with New Ways To Work. Good luck and let me know what happens.

According to Stoltz-Loike (1996), pointing out work realities is especially important when dealing with women. This is because, "Whether people are employed in academia, business, health professions or other fields, jobs are less secure and career paths more ambiguous" (p. 106). This means women need to plan strategically for their careers. Also, Stoltz-Loike noted "today, racism and sexism are much more subtle and take the form of denial of continued discrimination, antagonism toward the needs of women, and lack of support for policies structured to specifically assist women" (p. 106). Consequently, my response in the previous example addresses strategic planning and offers several resources for implementation.

Another difference between the two services is the definition of the word or concepts related to coaching. Generally speaking, both groups define *coaching* as mentoring, guiding or tutoring. However, as noted earlier in the NCDA's (1997a) publication on *Career Counseling Competencies, Revised Version, 1997*, the concept of coaching is much broader in scope. It suggests that counselors need to use their skills and influence for the greater good of society, by helping "the general public and legislators to understand the importance of career counseling, career development and life-work planning, (and) to impact public policy as it relates to career development and workforce planning." Furthermore, career counselors are expected to have the ability to "analyze future organizational needs and current level of employee skills and develop performance improvement training." Instead of expecting and holding an individual client accountable for performance improvement, the larger picture, scope or goal of this competency suggests "performance improvement" can be anticipated when the context of work and performance improvement training comes into play.

The definition of "coaching, consultation, and performance improvement," demonstrates a difference in the goals between the two services. Where coaching is primarily aimed at the individual, the field of career counseling aims at serving both the individual and society. The NCDA preamble specifies it is dedicated to the "enhancement of the worth, dignity, potential and uniqueness of each individual, and thus, to the service of society."

Other Differences

Other differences between coaching and career counseling involve professional preparation and training requirements. Certified career counselors are required to hold a master's degree in counseling or a related area such as human development. This academic training grounds them in career development theory as well as in "individual/group assessment skills considered essential for professionals engaging in career counseling" (NCDA, 1997a)." Assessment skills demonstrate the ability to:

1. Assess personal characteristics such as aptitude, achievement, interests, values, and personality traits.
2. Assess leisure interests, learning style, life roles, self-concept, career maturity, vocational identify, career indecision, work environment preference (e.g., work satisfaction), and other related life-style/development issues.
3. Assess conditions of the work environment (such as tasks, expectations, norms, and qualities of the physical and social settings).
4. Evaluate and select valid and reliable instruments appropriate to the client's gender, sexual orientation, race, ethnicity, and physical and mental capacities.
5. Use computer-delivered assessment measures effectively and appropriately.
6. Select assessment techniques appropriate for group administration and those appropriate for individual administration.
7. Administer, score, and report findings from career assessment instruments appropriately.
8. Interpret data from assessment instruments and present the results to clients and to others.

9. Assist the client and others designated by the client to interpret data from assessment instruments.
10. Write an accurate report of assessment results.

Another way to describe assessment skills utilized by qualified career counselors is described by Niles (1997) as "appraisal support" or helping clients identify their career concerns and/or barriers. Niles contended how a counselor intervenes with clients depends on an accurate diagnosis of the client's difficulty:

1. Decision-making difficulties caused by:
   a. dysfunctional beliefs
   b. lack of motivation
   c. insufficient information
   d. conflicts with occupational options
   e. Influence of a significant other
2. Work adjustment difficulties or adjusting to the work chosen is another area for exploration. This area addresses "the relationship between the worker and the work environment." The counselor's role in this case begins by assessing "whether the problem is related to work role behavior, task performance, worker satisfaction or some combination of these." For example: a. worker behaviors such as work addiction may best be remedied by attention to self-care, b. personality conflicts and disorders, are better treated by other resources and/or job support groups for this purpose, c. task performance issues relating to competencies may require remedial attention, on-the-job training, and/or continuing education, d. worker satisfaction issues may result from poor career choices and/or lack of goals.
3. World of work information including
   a. self-information: one's interests, skills, values, needs, and social or cultural context
   b. occupational information:
      1.) information on occupations
      2.) information on the nature of work and worker safety such as threats to health or economic security
      3.) Information on occupational strategies
         (a.) job hunting techniques
         (b.) career management/advancement strategies
            (1.) mentoring opportunities

(2.) career counseling support

(3.) ongoing self-assessment/development

(4.) creating individual career plans

(5.) continuing education

The list could be even longer. However, what's important about this list in terms of coaching and mentoring clients online is the attention to areas often overlooked, that is job hunting techniques and career management strategies are at the bottom not top of the list. This suggests that assessing the client's situation is primary in terms of assessment about what service to offer, what resources to refer, including the obligation to point out threats to a client's economic and/or physical health.

According to Niles (1997), it is important for career counselors to help the clients access accurate information about the world of work so they can make informed decisions. For example, many students and recent college graduates often take positions as cooks, waiters, or servers in restaurants. These jobs often go begging in many communities and offer young people a quick solution to earning steady income while job hunting for the ideal position, or in many cases, until they discover what they want. Although a temporary solution that has served many, it is a choice not without its risks to both health and long-term financial security. Niles noted:

> Threats to health include job related deaths, musculoskeletal injuries, and illnesses such as occupational cancers, occupational lung diseases, neurotixic disorders, hearing loss, and psychological disorders. Treats to economic security include poor wages, lack of health insurance, and lack of job security (p. 123)

Furthermore, Niles (1997) cited Jones, who suggested that clients need to consider these realities of work and learn how to protect themselves as well as how to "avoid viewing work as the primary source of self-esteem and meaning in one's life" (p.123).

Avoiding the view of work as a primary source of meaning in one's life is a difficult concept to convey to clients whether in person or online. This is one of the primary reasons clients seek assistance from career counselors even in times of full employment. This is why in times of full employment, when things don't happen as expected for clients, they ask: "What's Wrong with me?" For example, the following message is a case in point, with the client closing by stating, "there seems to be a lot of openings out there."

Dear Career Guru:

I'm not getting any interviews. What's wrong with me? I have been "searching" for well over a month. I respond to postings from numerous online services, talk to people on the phone, send faxes, interview at agencies, and have probably pursued over 300 positions for which I felt I was at least reasonably qualified. Recruiters have told me that I have "a good skill set," that I am "well qualified," and that it "shouldn't be hard to place" a person with my experience. So far, however, I have only had one interview with a "real" employer. I'm beginning to wonder if something is wrong with me. (Also, this doesn't seem like a very good time of the year to be searching for a job, although there seems to be a lot of openings out there.)

Reflecting on this message, I noted the client's difficulties may be a question of dysfunctional beliefs rather than difficulties within him. There may be nothing wrong with the client, meaning lack of motivation, performance, or skills set. His difficulty may rise from dysfunctional beliefs such as (a) thinking he could land a job in a month, (b) mailing 300 resumes cold or relying on recruiters for interviews, or (c) searching over the holidays, the worst time of year. These beliefs may be the reason he received only one interview from 300 mailed resumes. Or, it could be that this client needs a different recruiter, one specializing in his field. I address his beliefs first:

Here are a couple of things to consider. First, a month is not a long time to be searching for a job. It generally takes at least 3 months and with the holidays you might need to add 2 or 3 more. This is particularly true if you are sending resumes cold. Begin by trying some new search tactics. Instead of responding to hundreds of ads, limit your focus. Choose 10 to 12 companies or organizations you are really interested in. Research each carefully to learn about their mission, goals, products, and key players. By doing your homework, you'll uncover important information to include in cover letters. (The cover letter is one of the best ways to demonstrate your interest and knowledge to a potential employer.) Then network at professional meetings and with trusted colleagues who may open doors and advocate for you. And, instead of asking what's wrong with you, ask what's wrong with recruiters who say you "shouldn't be hard to place" yet turn up only one interview! I'd recommend finding a new recruiter. Also, don't stop searching because it's the holidays. Now is as good a time as any to search for a new job. In some ways, it's the best time because the holiday spirit can make people more open. It's also the best time to network because holiday parties and cel-

ebrations make networking more natural than at other times of the year. This may not be the best time of the year for receiving offers, yet there's no better time to lay your groundwork. Good luck!

Not every client writes back. Without client feedback, the online counselor has no way of knowing how his or her response was received. In this case, it may have been helpful to find out if a new recruiter solved the client's problem, or whether the client rethought his beliefs, choosing new job search strategies. There is the possibility that the response was not helpful, that learning a job search may take longer caused more discouragement.

Not knowing client outcomes plagues counselors who conduct in-person counseling equally, particularly with clients who attend only one session. Based on the high number of online clients who send thank you notes (one in seven), following one session, it appears online counselors may receive a higher percentage of feedback from their clients. This is why more research is needed to clarify what is meant by online career counseling versus career coaching and to examine client issues and outcomes generated by each service. In this way, we will know better if online career counseling is helpful or harmful. We will learn, too, which service is to be preferred for which issues or circumstances.

SUMMARY

Over the decades, new legislation aimed at addressing the needs of a changing workforce effected by plant closings, company downsizings, and corporate mergers paved the way for vast changes in the delivery of career counseling services. Government-sponsored one-stop career centers nationwide are one example. The rise of online career services marketed to a global population and the emergence of outplacement and career coaching services are others. Many leaders attribute the expansion of career services to counselors in the field who applied their coaching and consulting skills with key decision makers within communities and government agencies.

Although most associate the term *coaching* with mentoring, according to the *Career Counseling Competencies, Revised Version, 1997,* coaching encompasses a broad skills set including advocacy with the general public and legislators to impact public policy as it relates to career development and workforce planning. It also includes analyzing future organizational needs and current level of employee skills and developing performance improvement training. Coaching, usually associated with mentoring and advising activities, is but one aspect of this comprehensive skills set. Consequently, there is confusion about the terms used to describe online career services.

Until there is more clarity, I believe online career counseling, like WebCounseling, implies a deeper level of involvement with the client. Through graduate study, career counselors have knowledge and training in assessments, work-related issues effecting diverse populations, and a complexity of difficulties arising from dysfunctional beliefs including issues of health and safety in the workforce. In contrast, online career coaches restrict their expertise to job search issues or an information and referral model, providing clients with resources for their further investigation. Because many online clients also ask complex questions involving legal issues, paraprofessionals and commercial online career centers have found the need to create disclaimers and guidelines for what are and are not appropriate questions for an online format. These initiatives may prove equally beneficial for online career counselors.

DISCUSSION QUESTIONS

1. Define what is meant by the career competency: coaching, consultation, and performance improvements.
2. Compare and contrast online career counseling and online career coaching.
3. Give examples of when online career counseling may be more appropriate than online career coaching and vice versa.

6

Understanding the Use
of Assessment Online

"Aren't there tests to tell me what I'm good at ... I know I'd be good at something, but what?" Repeatedly, I heard this question when I began practicing career counseling at the Continuing Education Center for Women (CECW) located on the Campus of Indiana University Purdue University Indianapolis (IUPUI). Years later, clients both in person and online still ask about tests. Similarly, on behalf of OCC.com users, Susan Bryant and Craig Besant (respective product manager and vice president of marketing for OCC.com) asked: "Could you recommend some tests for clients or develop quizzes for online use?" Whether the question comes from individual clients or employers seeking tools to assist customers or employees, it demonstrates how closely the public identifies testing with career counseling.

The ACA clarifies the link between testing and counseling by purpose, noting: "The primary purpose of educational and psychological assessment is to provide measures that are objective and interpretable in either comparative or absolute terms" (section E.1.a). Interestingly, clients use these terms. They say things like "I want something objective to tell me" or "with a test, I'll be able to compare what I've been thinking with ..." Assessment, or what laypeople call *career testing*, has great appeal to both clients and counselors alike. For counselors, it can be a valuable tool in analyzing or determining issues, categorizing client difficulties, or providing the most appropriate referrals and links to additional resources.

CLARIFYING THE TERMS

The NCDA refers to "tests" by the term *assessment*, providing specific guidelines for counselors to follow. Guidelines cover the administration and interpretation of tests, as well as the specific guidelines for the use of computer-assisted instruments. Likewise the ACA and the NBCC detail their standards of practice under the titles *Evaluation, Assessment and Interpre*tation and *Measurement and Evaluation* respectively. Rather than discussing the specifics therein, for purposes of this discussion other distinctions regarding test terminology are highlighted, that is the difference between standardized tests and nonstandardized. According to Hansen, Stevic, and Warner (1976), standardized instruments are identified by four specific characteristics:

- A standard administrative process allows for similar administration and accurate measurement regardless of administrator or testing place or setting.
- Scoring instructors eliminate scorer errors so that regardless of the scorer the results are not influenced by personal bias.
- Normative data is available, allowing for comparison with diverse groups.
- A manual that includes technical testing data such as validity and reliability of the test instrument, is available so that the counselor can accurately decide if the test selected will measure or produce the most meaningful data.

Nonstandardized tests are assessments not sharing these characteristics. These may include brief quizzes or oral responses to questions meant to help individuals do their own self-evaluation. Other distinctions regarding tests include individual testing, group testing, paper-and-pencil tests, and online assessments. Whether "tests" are referred to as career tests, assessments, or instruments, standardized or nonstandardized, most counselors refer to them by category.

Categorizing Various Tests

Categories of tests generally include ability tests, aptitude, and achievement tests; interests or inventories and personality tests. A brief description of each follows:

1. Aptitude tests are intended to predict how well a person will do in an educational setting or perform on a job as measured by specific skills and proficiencies or the ability to acquire them.
2. Achievement tests assess the present levels of mastery or ability in academic skills such as arithmetic, reading, and language usage. They indicate areas of academic strength and/or areas in need of remediation.
3. Interest inventories measure interests in occupations, school subjects, leisure activities, and so on. Interest inventories are most closely associated with career counseling. The rationale behind these inventories is that individuals having similar interest patterns to those in an occupational group will probably find job satisfaction in that particular group. Three examples include the Strong Interest Inventory (SII), the Kuder Occupational Interest Survey, and the Self-Directed Search (SDS).
4. Personality inventories or tests encompass many variables such as self-concept and self-esteem, needs, values, interpersonal skills, emotional stability, risk-taking, motivation, and energy and level of maturity. Early researchers, like Roe, postulated that early personality development associated with family interactions influences vocational direction (cited in Zunker, 1994).
5. Values inventories classify values by categories such as intrinsic and extrinsic values or as work values, such as the need for power, money, achievement, prestige, security, creativity, etc. versus lifestyle values (home, family and leisure).

Self-assessment exercises or checklists allow clients to clarify specific skills and values on their own. Zunker noted that "more emphasis has been placed on skills identification through informal techniques" (p. 137). In addition to checklists and self-quizzes, card sorts are popular self-assessments, allowing the client to sort occupations, skills, and values, choosing or rejecting items by sorting into piles from *strongly agree* to *strongly disagree*.

THE ROLE OF TESTING THE COUNSELING PROCESS

Although all of these categories were an integral part of my graduate studies, fresh out of school, when asked about tests, I often replied that the best tests are self-tests. By this I meant the counseling process was primary to testing, it was its own type of assessment process. Exploration of career options and direction came by looking inside oneself, at one's hopes, dreams, and aspirations.

With a strong belief in Rogerian approaches to counseling, it was my contention that if clients had the opportunity to explore their concerns with a counselor, someone who would listen, nonjudgmentally, and provide feedback and resources, they would find their own way. Clients feeling heard, understood, and affirmed would be free to discover information on their own as well as appropriate resources (career and college information, financial aid, lists of local employers, salary surveys, etc.). By modeling a self-assessment process, clients would learn career management tools. In turn they would be able to articulate personal goals, define a direction, and choose the unique resources needed to overcome obstacles. My job was to provide a climate of trust, affirmation, and available resources. The administration of tests was not necessary to the equation. At that time, too, testing in general was somewhat suspect. It was a time when colleges actively recruited women and minorities by not requiring either college entrance or placement exams

Yet, as so often happened then and still happens with clients today, the general response to an introspective approach was, "that sounds nice, but I need to be realistic," meaning, "There are too many barriers for me to think about an ideal, I'm in a hurry. I haven't time to sit around or dream about what's best. I need a job." According to Hansen et al. (1976), Rogers also recognized this suggesting that "When tests come as a real desire from the client, they may enter the situation.... In this case the counselor's job is to focus on the client's feelings about the tests and its information" (p. 93).

The Career Counseling Process

Because I was often called on at CECW to give community presentations on the benefits of the career counseling, I developed a model to explain how it worked and why counseling instead of testing per se was helpful to clients. To make the process as simple as possible, I began by equating the counseling process with a series of questions similar to the six questions learned in high school English class about writing a good lead paragraph. Only I scrambled their order starting with *who, what, why, where, when,* and *how.* Then, I would draw a circle to demonstrate how the questions interact to create the career counseling process (see Fig. 6.1).

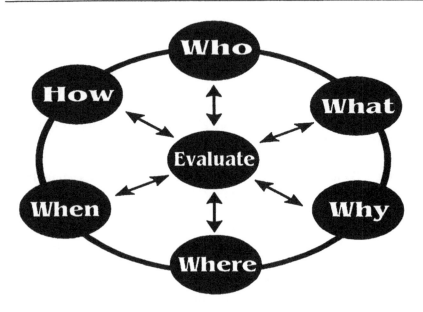

FIG. 6.1   Career counseling process (copyright © 1994 The Center for Career/Life Planning).

I would explain that questions related to *who*, *what*, and *why* are intrinsic to the client, that is they are concerned with the client's individual aspirations, skills, values, and lifestyle issues, or the context of the client's life. The *where*, *when*, and *how* questions are extrinsic to the client, focused on facts about careers, salaries, work environments, and job search techniques versus personal information. When the intrinsic questions are answered first, the others generally fall into place. For example:

- *Who* stands for questions related to client hopes, dreams, aspirations, or goals (for counselors, this includes asking about client expectations for career counseling). *Who* questions ask, "Who are you?" "Who do you want to be?" Because this population often denied, delayed, or buried their dreams, their most common response was: "That's why I'm here, I'm looking for direction."
- *What* refers to client skills, abilities, and personal traits. What they already have or what they want to develop. Often, clients would say they wanted to return to school but did not know what they wanted to study. *What* questions are designed to determine if more

schooling was necessary, particularly, if skills assessment showed a match for their goals (for the counselor, *what* questions help clarify the client issues versus presenting problems).

- *Why* questions determine client values or what is important to clients in terms of career satisfaction regarding job tasks, work environments, lifestyle concerns, and intrinsic and extrinsic rewards.

Next I would explain that answers to the *who*, *what*, and *why* questions demonstrate that the client, not the counselor, has the answers. The counselor is trained to ask the questions, reframe responses, and engage in a discovery process. I emphasize, too, that the first three questions are often the same questions (different words) asked by prospective employers in interviews (i.e., "Tell me about yourself," "What strengths and skills do you bring to the job," and "Why did you apply?"). In other words, the closer a client comes to answering these questions, the clearer the client's focus and better prepared for interviews whether for open positions or as candidates for graduate school. Audiences, like clients, understood the model easily, seeing its benefits by the explanation of extrinsic questions:

- *Where* refers to the importance of research to identify career options, job openings, and/or company information and salary surveys. This step includes the use of occupational and labor market information in the exploration of career options as well as interview preparation. In a job search, clients often skip this step. Career research is skipped or ignored because it is associated with long hours in the library. Although library research is perceived as tedious, I explain that research includes other tools like observation and interview techniques. For the job seeker with a clear direction, this means becoming aware of all the information that surrounds us daily, like spotting pertinent articles in the newspaper or feature stories on TV as well as networking with family, friends, colleagues, and peers for information.
- *How* relates to job search techniques such as developing professional networks, writing resumes and cover letters, interviewing and negotiation skills, and follow-up procedures. A large number of clients often enter career counseling with these concerns, and, more often than not are equally clueless about what they want to do. Consequently, the model becomes a frame of reference for the client to address the first three questions. And, in those rare

cases when a client is focused, conducts research, and truly needs help translating goals to paper, this step becomes the focus of the session.

- *When* questions are about decision making and include time lines and goal-setting. Because life rarely happens in neatly laid-out steps, decision-making questions are often the clients' presenting issues, particularly for those who plan to quit a job, return to school, or relocate. In those rare cases when everything appears to come together, many clients seek help exclaiming, "I'm so lucky, such and such just fell in my lap! Now I need to decide..."

To respond to issues of luck, I add the center circle to demonstrate the importance of choice and decision making. Like the arrows pointing to the center for evaluation, we have choices to exercise at any one point. When all six factors occur together, this is often called luck.

Instead of luck, I propose that a synergistic effect happens when we know clearly who we are or want to be, what we have to offer, and why it is important to us. When we also answer where we want to apply and how to present ourselves both on paper and in person, we are in the best position to evaluate our career options, choosing those that give us energy and/or new possibilities for continuing growth. Finding one's niche is not the result of luck, more often, it is the result of introspection and good career management skills.

Generally, audiences, like many clients, responded positively to these affective counseling methods talking openly about their earlier aspirations, and freely relating past successes and failures. They openly related personal circumstances such as a painful divorce, death of a spouse, loss of a child, or the under utilization of talents due to relocation, lack of opportunity in the workforce, discrimination, which all added up to unrealized or delayed dreams. In sessions, as I translated from their stories what I heard as their skill sets, personal traits, and new aspirations relating these to various career options to explore, discussions about tests diminished. As I watch clients moved forward, choosing to return to school, re-enter the workforce, advance in their careers, or choose to delay a decision, I became convinced that the career counseling process is its own assessment tool. And, as these clients referred others to us, as the demand for services grew with staff added to our center, I felt even stronger that self-assessment methods were best.

For me, the power of the career counseling process lay not in the sequence of questions asked or in formal testing, it was about being with the client. It was about attending to client feelings and facilitating a climate of trust allowing the client to make his or her own choices, find his or her own way. Yet as strongly as I believed in affective or insight counseling as an approach, I also recognized clients persisted in their requests for tests, wanting something concrete to confirm or deny their visions. I soon recognized that this population and indeed the general public found concrete or tangible results an affirmation in itself. And during the years since, I continue to see evidence that testing represents a type of affirmation for clients, particularly, when it confirms a vision of what they want to do, or helps them articulate a new direction. It is often one of the best starting points for the career counseling process. It is particularly appropriate as a starting point for the online career counseling process.

LESSON 7: AFFIRMING CLIENTS THROUGH ASSESSMENTS

Like many lessons along the road, my seventh lesson was relearning something I already knew, that is, clients say they feel affirmed by their test results. Affirmation appears to take place when the results of testing or an assessment session brings to light a client's strengths, new insights about preferences, and/or confirmation about new directions to pursue. Rarely does the client deny the tangible results from the testing, particularly, those articulating the client's potential. Having something tangible in black and white, so to speak, something that confirms an inner hunch or sparks an old dream, can be very energizing for clients. Testing provides hope as well as a starting point.

Client's View of Testing

According to Seligman (1980), some clients view testing as less threatening than counseling, using "a request for testing as a pretext for gaining access to personal counseling." And, Seligman holds that testing, if used, should be an integral part of the counseling relationship to:

- promote more relevant and focused discussion;
- stimulate and guide exploration and information-seeking;
- indicate the likelihood that certain events will happen;
- clarify self-concept;

- promote translations of interests, abilities, and personality dimensions into occupational terms;
- suggest options or alternative; and
- facilitate the ordering or ranking of options.

In other words, testing is a tool to help "summarize the responses of a given client and present them in a more useful form" (pp. 58–60). According to Seligman, the role of the counselor is to integrate the test data with other information the client has shared.

Since my early years as a career counselor, I have moved from focusing on client's feelings about the tests and test information to suggesting tests as a starting point. In the information age, many people struggle with information overload. Many clients describe themselves as confused. Others ask for help sorting through their options, and still others say they want a starting point. Testing is a tool to integrate career information into a personal decision-making process, thus assisting clients in focusing their priorities and moving forward. Although there are limits to the use of tests and assessment instruments, testing also helps counselors clarify client issues and difficulties and/or identify the most appropriate resources, referrals, and links. Testing also gives clients who are confused a starting point to identify or sort out difficulties. A case in point is illustrated by a high school math teacher, who signed his message, "Confused." Here is what he wrote:

> I have been teaching high school math since 1993, except for 1 year in which I worked as a statistical analyst for the actuarial department in an insurance company. I left teaching for that one year in hopes of finding something else that could be more overtly rewarding and financially more stable for my family. After working there for a year for approximately the same salary and being bored to tears by sitting in front of a computer calculating insurance rates all day, I went back to teaching. I realized I do my best work while dealing with people. I feel like I do a very good job teaching and have even won several awards for my teaching, including Outstanding New Classroom Teacher of the Year in my local district and Who's Who Among America's Teachers. Yet, with all of this, something is missing. I always wonder what if I was doing something else, or if I could even do something else which would make me feel the satisfaction I am looking for in a job. I also feel like I am not being personally challenged like I could be. I have sent resumes out and have it loaded onto several online services in hopes of hearing from someone who would offer me something that sounds like it would "fit."

However, I have yet to find many to take a bite and listen to me. I 'm
confused and financially stuck in the mud which is called public education or civil service with a wife and a newborn. What should I do???
Confused

Notice he states that he left teaching to find something "financially
more stable for his family." Later, he realized his best work is dealing
with people, returning to teaching where he knows he does a good job,
with national awards as evidence. Yet he finds something is still missing (obviously financial reward), but what? Obviously, too, he takes his
breadwinner role seriously, meaning financial considerations are a
priority along with job satisfaction. Notice, also, he leaves his career
choices to others. Suspecting his work values (job satisfaction vs. financial reward) are in conflict, I suggested the following assessments.

Dear Confused:
You may need another strategy. Instead of leaving the decision of the
right "fit" to online readers, define what you want. The Career Resource
page on the OCC site is designed to help you do this. Click:
<http://www.occ.com/occ/career/> and then link to the topics at the
top of this page. Begin with Self-Assessment and take the Values Identification Inventory and the Self-Directed Search. These are designed to
help you find a good fit by matching your interest and career values with
various positions. The next step is to learn more about appealing positions by reading details (working conditions, training, salary, employment outlook, etc.) in the 1998-99 Occupational Outlook Handbook at:
<http://stats.bls.gov/ocohome.htm>. Once you've completed these
steps, review the information under Career Search Basics, specifically, resumes and cover letters at: <http://www.occ.com/occ/career/basics/>.
By changing your strategies and taking charge of your career you should
begin to feel better and increase the likelihood of receiving a bite or two.
Good luck and keep me posted.

Here is another example. In this case, the client states clearly, "I just
need to know where to start." The message begins:

I've been in the IS field for 6 years now and I can honestly say that I de-
test it. I don't mean to offend any of you technical gurus, but this field
obviously is not for me. I had yet to complete my BA degree in Business.
I changed my major from MIS to Business a while ago because I just
couldn't grasp the concepts. Now, I'm contemplating a career change. I
just need to know where to start. I can't think of a single thing that I'm

actually pretty proficient in. Can you tell me what avenues to venture, if
any? Thanks ...

Because the client writes, "I can't think of a single thing I'm actually
pretty proficient in," asking "where to start," this is my clue to suggest
assessment. Since it is not clear whether he or she is currently enrolled
on campus, I offer more than one resource to pursue.

> The best way to start a career change is with assessment, finding out
> what interests you, what's important to you. Although you say you
> can't think of a single thing you're proficient in, there are probably
> many things you take for granted. So often what comes easily to us, we
> fail to recognize as strengths or skills. For example, not everyone is
> good at visualization ... picturing how a house will look after renova-
> tion or how a room will look with new furnishings. Some people do
> this naturally, never recognizing it's a skill required of architects and
> interior designers. Or some people are natural listeners. People gravi-
> tate to them to discuss problems or share secrets. You may be walking
> around with proficiencies you're not recognizing. If you are still in
> school, even part time, you should be eligible to use resources at the
> career services office of your college. Career counselors there will ad-
> minister a battery of vocational inventories to help you assess your
> strengths and focus your interests. Or check back to our site in an-
> other week when we will have assessment inventories available for
> your own self-assessment. Another indicator of avenues to venture
> can be found in your daydreams, daydreams of an ideal job. Spend
> some time daydreaming about what you'd do if money were no object?
> It may surprise you or give you direction about a major to follow. Good
> Luck and let me know if this helps.

Margaret Riley Dikel, a librarian, author, and recognized authority
on the use of the Internet as a tool in the career counseling process,
provides Internet resources and links through her Web site, The Riley
Guide. Dikel (1999) identified four categories of inventories, plus additional sources of Web sites for use in the career counseling process.
Assessment is ranked first. Notice how closely her list compares to the
various types of tests described earlier in the chapter. For example,
under assessments Dikel listed interest inventories, abilities/skills inventories, values inventories, personality inventories, and sources to
more tests.

Each of the categories highlight assessment instruments providing
direct links. Among the interest inventories, Dikel included, The Career Interest Game, which is based on the Holland's typology linked to

the host site, University of Missouri-Columbia at http://www.missouri.edu/~cppcwww/holland.shtml/; Find Your Career is based on the Campbell Interest and Skills Survey (CISS) offered by US News at http://www.usnews.com/usnews/edu/beyond/bccguide.htm/.

The Student's Center.com's About Work is also listed at http://www.aboutwork.com. However, since January 1999 the latter address for the Student Center links directly to Monster.com at: http://content.monster.com. This happened as the result of a merger among The Student Center, the Online Career Center, and MonsterBoard, the three becoming Monster.com. By combining resources, eight assessment links now are offered through Monster.com. To review these links, click at http://content.monster.com/tools/personality/links.html for a summary of what each offers below:

- *University of Waterloo Career Development Manual*: A comprehensive series of forms to organize your interests, values, and skills. Print out the career development manual pages, fill them in and review them regularly. Think of this as your career portfolio.
- *The Career Key*: A test that asks you to evaluate statements such as "I value science," or "I value arts" and yields six basic personality types. Career Key provides a long list of jobs that match the three types in which you score highest.
- *The Best Tests for Career Hunters*: More than two dozen different career-related quizzes have been gathered here. They address everything from sales jobs to owning your own business.
- *Kaplan Educational Centers*: Ten tests including the classic Kiersey Temperament Sorter, a time management test, and a job-readiness test.
- *Bowling Green State University Career Self Assessment*: A series of nonscored exercises that tell you how you want to live, what your skills are, and how to increase your self-awareness and self-confidence.
- *Online Personality Tests*: These tests are not scored but will teach you more about yourself. And the more you know, the more informed the choices you make will be.
- *TRIMA Career Competency Questionnaire*: A test that classifies personality traits and skills according to five types of competency, allowing you to determine your strengths and weaknesses in a work environment.

TESTING ONLINE: HOW IT WORKS

NCDA *Guidelines for the Use of the Internet for Provision of Career Information and Planning Services* are very clear about the Use of Assessment. Guideline 8., a–e specifies five conditions necessary for the use of online inventories or tests and their interpretation:

- The assessments must have been tested in computer delivery mode to assure that their psychometric properties are the same in this mode of delivery as in print form; or the client must be informed that they have not yet been tested in this same mode of delivery.
- The counselor must abide by the same ethical guidelines as if he or she were administering and interpreting these same inventories or tests in face-to-face mode or in print form.
- Every effort must be exerted to protect the confidentiality of the user's results.
- If there is any evidence that the client does not understand the results as evidenced by e-mail or telephone interchanges, the counselor must refer the client to a qualified career counselor in his or her geographic area.
- The assessments must have been validated for self-help use if no counseling support is provided, or that appropriate counseling intervention is provided before and after completion of the assessment resource if the resource has not been validated for self-help use.

The Strong Interest Inventory (SII) and Myers Briggs Type Indicator (MBTI) are two popular assessments used in career counseling. Although, not mentioned previously, both are standardized instruments, meeting NCDA criteria for administration and interpretation via the Web. For clients wanting more personal attention and/or standardized instruments measuring their interests and personal preferences, the SII and MBTI are often recommend. Clients are instructed to contact the (NBCC) at http://www.nbcc.org. In turn, NBCC offers referrals to qualified career counselors in the client's location. Qualified counselors are trained to administer and interpret these instruments, and to assist clients in understanding how to integrate results from the SII and MBTI with their work history, lifestyle, and personal circumstances. In response to the growing demand for career services, it is quite common to find many college and university career centers as well as private practitioners making administration of the SII and MBTI available via the web.

When clients choose the online option, the counselor combines e-mail counseling, telephone counseling ,and the online administration of the test instruments. Here's how it works. A client contacts the counselor by phone or e-mail asking for information about testing services. In turn, the counselor, either by phone or e-mail consultation, informs the client about the procedures. The client then makes an appointment. In some cases the client delays or declines the opportunity to make an appointment. When the client chooses the service, a time is set for an appointment (30–60 minutes) in which the counselor can conduct an intake interview. Generally the intake interview is conducted by phone. However, with an agreed on time, the appointment could also take place by e-mail with messages relayed between the two parties. The purpose of the intake appointment is for the counselor to achieve the following:

1. Interview the client for background information, goals, and expectations.
2. Assess the appropriateness of the instruments for the client.
3. Discuss fees and methods of payment for the service.
4. Provide the client access (log on name and password) for the secured site for test administration and scoring.
5. Set a mutually agreed on time for follow-up and interpretation.

As in any counseling situation, the intake stage is critical for both the client and the counselor. It is the counselor's job to establish a climate of trust for the client to share his or her concerns and for the counselor to assess the appropriateness of a testing procedure for the client.

In the two earlier examples, it is assumed the counselor established trust by posting her credentials as well as links to inform clients about her commitment to following *WebCounseling Guidelines*. It also is assumed that these clients, unlike those in face-to-face situations, have the opportunity to observe the counselor's style and expertise by reading previously posted online messages. By posted messages, I refer to those posted daily on OCC.com and Netscape.com during the months of August 1998 through January 1999. Although the messages were posted anonymously, the high number of individuals signing first and last names to their original questions gives further evidence of counselor trust.

If, as Seligman (1980) suggested, testing is "a pretext for gaining access to personal counseling," it is the counselor's obligation to inform clients they may not benefit from testing. In these cases, the counselor makes other or more appropriate recommendations and/or referrals for the client to pursue. After the counselor offers appropriate resources, it becomes the client's responsibility to accept or reject the referrals and/or recommendations. For example, when clients ask for assessment or suggestions to get started, instead of testing, other resources may be suggested. Sometimes career counseling is not what the client needs. Simply, a request for testing may be the pretext for reaching out. A case in point is the following woman who wrote for suggestions:

> I am 40 and single with no savings. I have worked in low paying jobs due to my interest in the arts and community/service-oriented organizations. I have a BFA in modern dance and a masters in international business from Thunderbird (American Graduate School of International Management). My family is very concerned about my financial and career future—namely benefits and retirements. I have not worked at any one job longer than two years due to a variety of reasons (mainly geographical moves). I don't want to sell my soul but I do want some security. Any suggestions?

Notice the client's love of her field as evidenced by her work history in the arts and her statement, "I don't want to sell my soul." However, by the latter statement one can assume she has fallen into the trap that the arts do not pay well. Testing in her case may not be appropriate. Instead, it may be more appropriate to provide referrals that meet her need to become financially secure. These referrals could include a financial planner and/or links to other online information about alternative opportunities in the arts. As a counselor, I also want to affirm her earlier choices by writing:

> You are to be commended for using your education in your life's work! I know many with large savings accounts who'd envy you that. On the other hand, you are wise to think about your future and now is not too soon. Start by finding a good financial planner, one who is fee-based, who gives advice rather than sells products. To find one in your area, contact the Institute for Financial Planners, at http://www.icfp.org/. This site has a database you may search for a financial planner in your area of

the country. A financial planner will assure you there is still time/years to prepare for your future. And, you don't have to sell your soul to do it in an unsuitable job. I know many people in the arts who administer arts programs within government service. They are paid well, have benefits, and are able to build for their future. Foundations and endowments for the arts offer other opportunities to work in your profession while building financially. Some of the highest paid executives in our country work for foundations, many of which dispense large grants for the arts. You can investigate this possibility by visiting the Foundation Center online at http://www.fdncenter.org/. Good luck and I hope this information helps. Sincerely, Dr. Patricia Boer, OCC's Career Guru

Just as counselors look for confirmation regarding their feedback to clients by observing the client's verbal and nonverbal messages, the online counselor verifies by the client's return message. In this case, the client wrote back almost immediately stating:

Thank you very much for your advice. It was just what I needed today. I will look into your suggestions. It was very helpful and encouraging. All the best.

SUMMARY

And, as the client in these messages writes, "It was just what I needed today ... very helpful and encouraging." Sometimes that's all the client is really looking for, something helpful and encouraging or "just what I needed today." Client messages like this example and similar ones highlighted earlier, such as those expressing feelings of "being more relaxed," "getting a grip," "gaining peace of mind," and so on, indicate the power of brief counseling.

These messages also imply the importance of assessment, pointing out that assessment is not always an instrument. In the larger picture, assessment is the counseling process itself, with test instruments supplementary, providing a useful way to explain client issues. Testing as a tool of the larger process provides clients with a starting point. Testing often affirms the client by confirming an aspiration or providing the motivation to move forward. However, testing has its limitation and by itself does not address individual differences, including cultural differences, the structure of opportunity, institutional sexism and/or racial, gender, sexual orientation, and age discrimination. These issues are more fully developed in the next chapters.

DISCUSSION QUESTIONS

1. What is your definition of assessment?
2. Define and describe the link between testing and career counseling.
3. Which tests are of most benefit to career counseling clients?
4. When is testing not appropriate for a career counseling clients? Why or Why not?
5. Name and discuss online Web sites and resources for career assessment.

7

Providing Appropriate Information and Referral

If there is any argument demonstrating that online services extend access and provide a unique service for what professionals call special populations, it is illustrated by the fourth competency for certified career counselors, that is, information resources. To become familiar with the vast array of resources and understand which is the most appropriate for which individual or special population is a skill in itself, particularly in an age of specialization. For example, providing the most appropriate referrals for a person with a disability is very different from those specific to the Asian American community (illustrated in chap. 4) versus the gay and lesbian community, or discrimination issues related to gender, race, culture, ethnicity, and/or ageism.

NCDA DEFINITION

According to the *Career Counseling Competencies, Revised Version, 1997,* the fourth of the career counseling competencies calls for:

> Information/resource base and knowledge essential for professionals engaging in career counseling. Demonstration of knowledge of: (1) Education, training and employment trends; labor market information and resources that provide information about job tasks, functions, salaries, requirements and future outlooks related to broad occupational fields and individual occupations. (2) Resources and skills that clients utilize in life-work planning and management. (3) Community/professional re-

sources available to assist clients in career planning, including job search. (4) Changing roles of women and men and the implications that this has for education, family, and leisure. (5) Methods of good use of computer-base career information delivery systems (CIDS) and computer-assisted career guidance systems (CACGS) to assist with career planning.

EXAMPLES OF MULTIPLE ISSUES FROM ONLINE PRACTICE

The importance of this competency, providing appropriate information and referrals, is all the more important when someone's circumstances call for information in multiple areas just cited or when the person represents more than one special population. This is why I believe working online requires experienced counselors with a strong knowledge base and understanding of special populations. Client examples illustrate my point.

Client Messages

A message referred from Netscape, another Web site, is a case in point. The Netscape representative wrote OCC.com requesting that I respond, noting:

"This came in over the wire. I am at a loss in terms of how to answer this person. Perhaps this could be something for the career guru. Sort of a sad e-mail that I would love to get a reply off to, but I don't know what to say. Thanks for your help." Here's the client's message:

Example 1: Displaced Homemaker

I would like to know what choices there are for those who are totally out of touch with what is going on in the world. I am 47 years old, was married most of my life, am legally blind and a returning student at Cal State University. I am not sure what I can do because I have never done anything in the job field. I have taught ESL in Mexico and worked slightly as a teacher's aid in USA, but with my bad eyesight that possibility is becoming less feasible. I have access to reading machines, called a CCTV, but it is not portable. Transportation is also a problem. Are there any tests that someone can take that would place one in a particular job field or possible type of work? It would also be nice to have a list of tasks required in a certain job, for example, a secretary needs to type at least 40 words a minute, take shorthand or dictation, do filing and be good with people. I know that there are a lot of things a person would be good at if only there was *a guide as to what kind of job the person could qualify for just from life ex-perience. I refuse to think that all my years of experience have taught me nothing that could help me find a job.*

Notice the layperson from Netscape picked up on the feelings expressed by the writer, characterizing the message as, "Sort of sad e-mail." Notice, too, there is more than one presenting issue for the client, regarding world of work information (i.e., being out of touch with the world of work, being a person with a disability, having a transportation problem, and not knowing how to translate her skills and life experiences into paid employment). Seemingly unaware that attendance at Cal State entitles her to multiple university services, she asks, "Are there any tests?"

As a counselor, it is also my job to both respond to her question and point out resources at her university. It is also my job to instruct her about the meaning of *job accommodations* in order to address her transportation problems and visual impairments. Here's my response:

Since I am a career counselor, your message was forwarded to me for a reply. You are wise to be among the returning students at Cal State. This is one of the best ways to get back in touch as well as prepare to re-enter the workforce. And, yes, there are many tests to identify or match you interests, experiences, skills, and values with appropriate occupations. Here are resources to contact:

1. Career Services Office on-campus at Cal State. Career testing is one of the services offered to students through your campus. Call there for an appointment. You are right, too, about life experience teaching us many things. Colleges, today, recognize this and offer what's called life experience credit as well as offer students the opportunity to test out of courses. Ask the counselors at the career center about this.

2. State Vocational Rehabilitation. Another option for you is to take vocational tests in your community through the state's Vocational Rehabilitation Services. Since you wrote that you are legally blind, you may be eligible for a full array of Vocational Rehabilitation services, which fall under the Americana with Disabilities Act (ADA). This means the law is on your side and you could be eligible for disability benefits, vocational training, and reasonable accommodations by employers.

3. Job Accommodation Network (JAN). Accommodations mean not only adaptive devises, like the CCTV you mentioned, but accommodations include a person to read or drive for you. For specific information about your situation, contact the Job Accommodation Network (JAN) at 800–526–7234. JAN offers free consultations.

4. The Campus Adaptive Services Office. Or, start on campus by making an appointment with a counselor in Adaptive Services Office. A counselor there will help you prioritize and coordinate all available services including those offered at the Career Services Office on-campus or in your community.

5. Vocational Tests. What you want is a battery of vocational assessments to help you determine the best career matching with your interests, skills, and values. You'll also want assistance identifying appropriate accommodations so that you can work toward developing a career, not just a job. By finding the right resources and learning more about all your choices, you will find your niche as well as ways to use all the experience life has taught you.
Good luck and I hope this helps.

I never heard from this woman. Most counselors will tell you that one of the problems responding to clients with information versus attending skills is that the technique may backfire. Information can overwhelm the client who is not ready to hear it or take action. This was not the case in the next client example.

Example 2: Unemployed Person

I am just completing a program for those disabled and unemployed. My disability is a hearing loss.(I can use a telephone, though not while wearing an aid.) My skills are now thorough knowledge of Word97, Excel97 and taking courses on ZD University. Access and soon hope to master Visual Basic or VBA. My typing skills are 45+, though I do freeze up under testing. I enjoy a varied busy day, though one not overwhelming. Also enjoy helping others. I taught Bridge (card game) and really enjoyed my work day. Though in Florida almost every bridge teacher moved or settled here. Thank you. Merry Christmas

P.S. I have my B.A. from NYU. in Business Administration, and minor in Accounting. I also have strong Math skills, people skills, and passed the Word97 and Excel97 with flying colors.

In this message, the client's tone is very positive, filled with the pride of accomplishments. He describes himself as "enjoyed a varied busy day ... enjoyed my work day ... also have strong Math skills, people skills and passed ... with flying colors," and even wishes me Merry Christmas! Yet, notice, he does not ask a question per se. He implies he needs help with employment. And, like the woman in the former example he appears not to know he may have access to resources through his university, or in his case his alma mater. Not knowing exactly what he wants, I replied:

> If you're writing about changing careers, I'm surprised you're not receiving assistance through the program you are completing presently. If there are no placement services available there, check with your alma mater, NYU. The university may offer direct career assistance to former graduates. You may link to the NYU career center at http://www.nyu.edu/careerservices/>. Counselors at the career center can coach you on the basics of changing careers and put you in touch with companies seeking their graduates. Or, link back to the NYU home page to connect and network with alumni members. You may find job openings to work for the University which is an option you might consider, too. Since you like to help people, state you are good at math, with a degree in business, and minor in accounting with computer expertise as well, you have the makings of a great financial aid officer. Or you may want to use your new computer skills in the Adaptive Technology Department, helping other hearing impaired students to better access the resources of the university. Hopefully, too, you'll find NYU, like many universities, gives employment preference to people with disabilities. Good luck and let me know if this helps.

This client wrote back immediately indicating my responses were on target, indicating the information was not overwhelming. It helped:

> Thank you for your fast reply. I am presently interning at Miami-Dade Access Dept assisting low vision students with their term papers, using the talking computers. And, tutoring students in remedial math. It takes close to two hours each way to commute, so I had not given it any thought. As I am now in Florida, I did not think about asking at a New York College. I will contact NYU and look into all that you have informed me. Thank you. Have the happiest holiday ever!

Even Ivy League-educated medical students have concerns and seek information.

Example 3: Medical Student

> O.K. Here's a doozy ... I'm a medical resident that not only is fearful of his job since managed care is lingering around, but also one in a great deal of federal educational debt. I am discovering, however (through various tests and books) that I am not truly happy with what I do. I feel I

need to flex my creative side more, and will only be happy doing so. I have been classified as "ENFP", and I feel this is a very accurate description. I really want to change careers, but I have to pay off my loans. What do you suggest ... stick it out and pay them off (10–15 yrs) or be oblivious and go for it? Help!!

Here's my response:

Yes, it's always a doozy when the decision is posed as an either/or situation. These types of decisions generally add to feelings of being stuck. To change that, use your creative side to think about options within the medical field. This way you will draw on all you've learned rather than be oblivious to it. For example, the success of the TV series ER is attributed to its author, Crichton, who used his experience as a student at the Harvard Medical School when he logged innumerable hours in the Massachusetts General Hospital emergency room working toward his degree as a medical doctor. During that time, he was also beginning to make his way as a writer and, in fact, paid his way though medical school writing paperback thrillers. Just as ENFP's make good writers and/or journalists, they also make good psychologists, psychiatrists, teachers, and practitioners of holistic or alternative medicine as well as management consultants. Why not look for ways to integrate medicine into one of these areas, or in the emerging field of fundraising and development. Professionals who direct medical foundations are well paid. To investigate foundation careers link to The Foundation Center at http://www.fdncenter.org. And, if none of these suggestions appeal to you, invest a few hours with a qualified career counselor who will help you explore other options. Contact the National Board for Certified Counselors at http://www.nbcc or make an appointment online with Career Development Services, Rochester (CDS) NY, NY, which offers a very reliable service in partnership with the Wall Street Journal at http://www.careers.wsj.com. By expanding your options, you'll make a better decision and formulate a plan you'll be happier with. Good luck and let me know if this helps.

Within 48 hours, the client wrote back ... from the tone, you can almost feel his excitement and appreciation for a burden lifted, for the discovery of new options and resources to pursue.

Wow ... just wanted to say thanks for your advice ... it certainly helped me make some initial decisions ... is there a phone number or more direct way to access your services? Are you an individual or do you have

others working for you (pref. in the Cinci, OH region?) Thanks again, I
will forward your name to many others.

EXPERIENCE FROM CCLP/PRIVATE PRACTICE

It may be important to note that all examples in the book were selected
from messages sent to me directly before they were publicly posted. I
read and responded to each, allowing clients to respond in kind. OCC
provided this service at no charge to the job seeker (850 clients who
utilized OCC.com). In contrast, once OCC merged with Monster I was
listed among the experts on the message boards where questions or
messages were posted publicly instead of arriving at my private practice, Center for Career/Life Planning (CCLP). As a courtesy for clients
wanting to hire my services, Monster provided a direct link to CCLP.
Naturally, I appreciated this, as career counseling is both my profession and the way I make my living. However, it rarely worked that way.
Monster clients appeared to use the link to bypass the message boards
and chats in the hopes that I would answer directly. So, I would respond by noting they had reached my private practice, a fee-for-service
program, and directed them back to free services at Monster or suggesting they search for one-stop centers in their community at
http://www.ttrc.doleta.gov/onestop.

There are three interesting points about these clients: (a) confidentiality did not appear to be an issue, meaning, this was not the motivation to link to my private practice; (b) they shared a great deal of
personal information either anticipating I would answer and/or expecting CCLP to be a free service; and (c) only a small percentage (less
than 2% or 28 from an estimated 1,440 e-mails) contracted for paid
services with CCLP. This led me to conclude that only a small portion
of the public is ready to pay for online service, particularly when free
services are readily available.

I also concluded that it was not fair to provide free services to those
linking through Monster when my in-person clients were paying for
similar privileges. At times, I felt torn. There were so many messages
and with resources at my fingertips, a brief reply would not hurt them
or me. I did this initially before joining Monster, and until the brief
messages took more time than those I answered for Monster or spent
conducting live chats. It was then I began using a cut-and-paste
method. Yet, every now and then one or two of messages would stand
out, giving me pause. This is one such message. As you read it you'll see

why I responded, ever briefly, and why I believe providing information and referral is important online service.

Example From CCLP/Private Practice

Notice the message is from a 53-year-old male following a downsizing or "reduction in force" (potential discrimination/ageism issue). He asks about employer background checks (legal issue) adding he has multiple sclerosis (a disabling disease). Here is his actual message and with his permission, his signature.

> I am a 53-year-old male who was just gone through a "Reduc-tion-in-Force". To date I have sent out over 125 resumes to viable job of-fers for which I was uniquely qualified. So far … I have received only ONE positive response for future consideration, only to be told that the employer has just instituted a "Hiring Freeze. " Several of my fellow younger associates, who were also let go, have already received several valid job offers within our computer software/business analyst industry.

> Additionally, I have read recently where employers are now using private "Investigation Search" firms for background screening information of ap-plicants. There are laws that restrict what kinds of information (job re-lated only) an employer can elicit from the applicant, yet there appears to be no such safeguard for the potential employee in regard to these "Investigation background checks?"

> Another concern that impacts my employment situation is the fact that I have Multiple Sclerosis, which was first discovered back in 1965. The dis-ease has taken a toll on my ability to walk without assistance, but other than the damage that has already occurred I am one of the "Lucky" MS survivors who can still lead a somewhat normal existence. Over the last five years I have not missed ONE single workday due to an ailment of any kind. BUT … if a prospective employer finds out that I DO have MS … guess who will NOT be offered a job??

> Perhaps I am just going through some sort of normal job search para-noia, but it would appear that someone in my shoes (being over 50 and having a so-called catastrophic disease) has only a remote chance of ever getting another job for which I am truly qualified???

In addition to the issues this client presents, his message also illus-trates the amount of personal information clients are willing to share online, even before they contract for services. Like many clients, he freely provides personal details about his age, education, and disability. Like many, too, he asks *what's wrong with me*, "am I just going through some sort of normal job search paranoia?"

Because I was traveling the day his message arrived, it posed an added challenge. Was this a question I really wanted to ignore or could I quickly send a brief response from my laptop? Sometimes, too, a client truly seeks my services and might be insulted if I assume he or she is writing only for free services. Monster.com does clearly provide on my bio page, the link for inquiries about my private practice, the CCLP. As is seen here, I wrote him, mentioning my services, fees, and procedures with a brief postscript. And, notice I respond to only one of his three issues, very briefly, too. This is definitely not an example of on-line career counseling, it is strictly an example of providing accurate information and referral. However, it does demonstrate how empowering the right information can be for a client.

My Reply

Thank you for inquiring about my private practice, which is a fee-for-service program. If you are interested in these services I would be happy to assist you. I've helped many clients long distance. Below are details about my online services, fees, and procedures. You may read details below or the general information on my vocational testing site at http://admin.cpp-db.com/C/cclpin. Sincerely, Pat Boer

P.S.
Because you have M.S., consider calling the Job Accomodation Network (JAN) for additional suggestions and advise. There is no charge for this service and it may be the best call you'll ever make. If you do and it helps, let me know. The number is (1–800–526–7234, outside West Virginia and inside the state at: 1–800–526–4698)

The Client's First Reply

Your prompt reply is most excellent! I will contact JAN as you suggested and proceed onward from that point. The additional information about your services is impressive and the fee structure is reasonable. After I have contacted JAN, I will get back to you with the results and the next step in my quest for continued employment. Your kindness is much appreciated … Jim Minehan

A month later he wrote about his experience with JAN ....

Client's Second Reply

Last month (11–11–99) you were kind enough to E-mail me some information about your services and also suggest that I contact the Job accommodation Network (JAN) for assistance with my search for new employment based on the fact that I have MS. In your note back to me you suggested that contacting JAN might be a most valuable tool for me and your advice was 100% ACCURATE. Please allow me to say THANK YOU in a big way for your suggestion.

I spoke to a man named Eddie at JAN last week and explained that I was afraid my MS was being used against me by many of the respective new employers that I had been in contact with. Eddie took the time to talk me through all the potential options and variables that I might encounter. During the course of our conversation, Eddie mentioned the fact that he was born without any arms. Needless to say, my perceived troubles suddenly took a back-seat position. The person to whom I was speaking was recording my pertinent information by typing on his keyboard with his TOES!I was truly impressed with Eddie's demeanor and candor as he so generously assisted my situation and responded with valuable information that I can use most effectively on a going forward basis. I have such respect and admiration for someone like Eddie who has overcome a situation that is unthinkable in most people's realm.

Thanks to Eddie (and ultimately … yourself) I can get back on track and focus on the real blessings that I do have and continue with my quest for new employment with a renewed enthusiasm!!!

I truly hope you have an excellent holiday season and Happy New Millennium! Certainly I will … thanks to your excellent assistance.

Most Sincerely,
Jim Minehan

My Second Reply

As I have noted throughout this book, I've received many notes of appreciation. Jim's stands out among the top five. Not only is he appreciative of the information, he generously shares how he's used it. His message demonstrates how one unknown resource (JAN) can make a major difference in a person's life. It also reminds me of something a colleague used to say in training sessions regarding appropriate information. Here's my paraphrased version, "sometimes, with new information the very thing we want to fight and die for on Friday, becomes what we want to live for Monday."

When new information is the client's main issue, helping him or her access the information or providing the appropriate link is key. Access is what online career counseling provides, yet many counselors are still skeptical of this medium. This is why I asked Jim for permission to share his experience, writing.

Dear Jim!
I am so glad to know JAN was helpful to you. And, thank you for writing back such a warm and complete update. I know it took thought and time so I appreciate that too. It also was inspirational to read. Now, I'm wondering if I could ask a favor of you. I am writing a book for counselors on the value of e-mail career counseling and would like to include your message as an example of how this medium reaches out and is helpful to more people than our traditional delivery methods (in-person). It my belief the Internet is a valuable tool to extend services, particularly, for people with disabilities or anyone who might hesitate to meet with a counselor face to face. Let me know if you would be willing to share your message. Your name can remain anonymous like the other messages I present, or adding it may demonstrate that many users do not worry as much as professionals about confidentiality. Please do not feel you have to say yes. If you prefer not to be in the book I understand totally. Thank you again for writing back. Your appreciation made my day and makes all my work worthwhile. A very happy holiday to you too!!!
Pat

Here's his permission:

I would be honored for you to use my response in your book! You also are absolutely correct about the positive impact of E-Mail career counseling. It DOES work. Please let me know when the book is published so I can be one of the first to get a copy. You are obviously very gifted at what you do and the book has to be of equal quality. If you ever get out to Arizona on a book signing tour I can have you autograph it. Thank you for ALL you have done for me!!!
Jim

My reply

Thank you for your written permission to include your example and words in my upcoming publication on career counseling over the Internet. Once, published I'll personally make sure you're among the first to receive a copy. Now it's my turn to say thank you. Thank you, Jim, I truly appreciate your assistance and know your voice will have an important and positive influence on readers.
Best regards, Pat

Looking back on this scenario, I gained much, too. I learned you don't need to respond to everything to be helpful to a client. Sometimes, underneath the story is one factor driving the others. When that's addressed, the client handles the rest. It's an important lesson for this online art, and a reminder of what I learned years ago as a practicum student. I can still hear my supervisor say, "Clients tell you what's important in the first 5 minutes. If you miss it, they'll tell you again until you get it or they move on to another counselor." As I would review tapes for submission or later from students presenting their tapes to me, I would hear the client say from the beginning what was important. Jim's message teaches me anew, leading me to my eighth lesson on the road.

LESSON 8: PROVIDING APPROPRIATE ONLINE INFORMATION AND REFERRAL

What makes the skill of online information and referral important is the word *appropriate*. Messages needn't be long or detailed, as in my message to Jim. Messages simply need to match the client's chief concern. And, they needn't come from extensive online searches. Appropriate information and referral is often drawn from experiences the counselor brings to the online setting, from his or her previous in-person practice. This was the case with both Jim and in the earlier example with the medical student.

Brevity may also be important and reinforces one of the dos and don'ts recommended for career coaches. In a training model developed for online career coaches, Louann Kummerer, senior consultant for Interim Career Consulting, Inc., now Spherion Corporation, emphasizes, "You don't need to over answer." As I look back on so many of my early responses I wonder if over answering isn't my weakness. It's so easy to do. It's like giving too much feedback in a face-to-face session when you need to be listening. Listening is equally important when clients ask of information about education, training and employment trends.

GETTING STARTED WITH ONLINE INFORMATION AND REFERRAL

So how do career counselors who want to practice online know which sources are the most appropriate for referrals for clients, particularly those representing diverse populations or who ask complex questions related to disability issues, ageism, and the legal ramifications? Basically, you do it the same way you would offer referrals to clients in person. You begin with the basics.

Using Labor Market and Educational Information

Most career counselors are familiar with and refer clients to labor market information published by the U.S. DOL such as the Dictionary of Occupational Titles (DOT) at http://www.oalj.dol.gov/libdot.htm or what's now called O*Net at http://www.doleta.gov/programs/onet/. The Occupational Outlook Handbook (OOH) is another DOL publication at http://www.bls.gov/ocohome.htm. It works the same way for information on education. Many counselors rely on Peterson's Guide. This guide is also available online at http://www.petersons.com.

Using the NCDA Site

Another way to get started is by finding a site with established and extensive resources for referral. Just as many counselors might turn to the NCDA for printed resources to provide clients or add to their personal career libraries, these resources are available online on the NCDA homepage at: http://www.ncda.org/hotlinks.html/.

NCDA Links.   The links on this page not only connect to the OOH, there are links to:
- state labor market information: http://www.dbm.com/jobguide/trends.html#gov/
- community colleges and universities: http://www.utexas.edu/world/univ/
- financial aid: http://www.ed.gov/proginfo/SFA/StudentGuide

Other links are categorized under organizations and publications; career planning and assessment; searching databases for occupational information education and training, financial aid, internships, and job openings, as well as links to other online career centers. By identifying lists of links such as those available on the NCDA site, valuable time can be saved. These are not the only links to recommend. NCDA represents just one starting point. For financial aid, I like a very simple site call Find Aid at http://www.finaid.org. However, the value of starting an online search by using a site like NCDA is the information has already been sorted for ease of retrieval.

NCDA Publication.   Another tool to help the novice get started is the NCDA (1998) publication, *The Internet: A Tool for Career Planning*. This first edition lists a model for career planning as well as sample websites developed by Dikel. This publication was not in print when I started online, so today's novice may very well want to begin with its review.

Using Resources on NACE

The National Association of Colleges and Employers (NACE) offers one of the most complete list of resources. It is easy to use with the alphabetized list at http://www.jobweb.org/map.htm. More than 50 resource links are available for clients and counselors to search for their own college career center, internships, information on headhunters and search firms as well as company information and job trends. Counselors who are familiar with or who have referred in-person clients to NACE publications, like Job Choices, will find this online resource even more valuable.

Using Monster.com

Another way to get started is the way I did. You begin with one of the online centers, which provides extensive information and/or links to labor market trends, salary surveys, relocation information, and databases you can search by city, state, country, and industry.

CREATING USEFUL INDEXES OF RESOURCES

Utilizing any and all of the above ways to get started will help the novice find his or her own favorite links and resources. Also, I have compiled a basic list of links to help the novice get started online. The resources/links are categorized links by

1. Career counseling for referrals to career counselors in person.
2. Education and training for referrals to educational information, alumni groups, and financial aid.
3. Internships to refer career changers as well as traditional students.
4. Occupational information about various career options.
5. Job openings to search nationwide including a list of the 200 best small companies.
6. Military career guides for career transition.

These categories are incomplete and something I put together to help me get started. Once you go online, you'll find your own. You'll notice this basic list is just that. It's very basic and does not include lists for special populations. This is because I discovered the Society for Human Resource Management (SHRM) has compiled one of the best lists of resource links on special populations at http://www.shrm.org/hrlinks. These links give special attention and resources to complex issues and special populations including the following

- Diversity issues and affirmative action.
- Flexible work arrangements.
- Expatriate worker.
- Safety and health issues including employee assistance programs, sexual harassment, and workforce violence.
- Work/life with 14 separate links including issues on the best companies for women and minorities, elder care, day care and the family and medical leave act.

Further, Monster.com compiled specialized lists under Toolkits for:

- Women workers at http://content.monster.com/womenworkers/
- Older workers at http://content.monster.com/olderworkers/
- Military transition at http://content.monster.com/military/
- International at http://international.monster.com/workintheus/

In addition there are many more links for resources covering issues I have not mentioned, such as mentoring and employee assessment and links for the gay and lesbian community. Instead, this is an overview or guide to get started. Once comfortable online, the second stage for learning about appropriate links for information and referral happens by searching online and toggling back and forth until you find what fits. At this stage, some counselors may want to take computer courses to help them feel more proficient online. I took several courses that helped me feel more confident about my process and how I maneuvered online.

However, it wasn't computer courses or searching online that lead me to resources like JAN. I'd like to say I discovered this resource by searching online, like I did with SHRM at http://www.shrm.org. However, that's not the case. My knowledge of JAN (http://janweb.icdi.wvu.edu/english/contact.htm) grows from experience providing a diverse population with information and resources. One excellent resource is a book by Melanie Astaire Witt (1992), *Job Strategies for People with Disabilities*, pertinent for special populations today.

EXAMPLES OF ADDITIONAL RESOURCES

Some resources that did result from online searches are related to special populations and warrant attention. Here's one on discrimination based on sexual orientation, signed, "Thanks, I hope!!" He writes:

> I'd appreciate some advice from people who are or have experienced job loss due to discrimination based on sexual orientation, sexual harassment, and other similar reasons. How do you cope during the legal "battle", how do you regain your self esteem and self-confidence. When do you stop being angry and feeling like a victim? What do you do when you transfer out of state for a promotion that turns into a "nightmare" such as described above? Hope you get my drift; I can assure you even a monetary settlement is meaningless when you've suffered any of the above experiences. Thanks, I hope!!!

Although my response may look like it gives this client several options, it may be an example of overanswering or overwhelming a client. As counselors know, many clients just want a safe place to vent rather than information or problem-solving strategies. It is possible that someone going through litigation just wants to sound off or find support. This is why my response starts with a referral to a career counselor as a first step in seeking support and exploring options:

> Yes, psychological pain and grief are always harder to experience and handle, making monetary settlements seem unimportant. Like handling any type of grief, begin by acknowledging that it's hard and accept your feelings as okay. To do this takes understanding and support from friends, family, and professionals, even your attorney. Keep in mind, too, it's always harder to feel okay when your future seems uncertain. So make support your first goal. Find a qualified counselor by contacting the National Board of Certified Counselors at http://www.nbcc.org. Once you deal with your grief and feelings, the second part is easier, that is, discovering new options. As you begin to discover new choices, you'll feel less like a victim and find your self-esteem and confidence return. To explore all your options for support and future employment check out these Web sites:

1. The Gay Workplace Issues Homepage at
   http://www.nyu.edu/pages/sls/gaywork. On this page you'll find resources for organizations, company policies, universities, publications,
   and e-mail lists.
2. The National Organization for Gay and Lesbian Scientists and Technical Professionals at http://www.noglstp.org. If you are in a technical
   field this is a good place to start. This site has a workplace discussion
   list, and/or workplace issues.
3. Company lists and links to the 100 most positive companies for gays,
   lesbians, and bisexuals at http://www.noglstp.org/. By developing a
   supportive network and researching companies with work environments matching your interests and orientation, you will both feel
   better and avoid another nightmare. Good luck and let me know if
   this helps.

Or consider this request from a woman looking to make a career
change from education. She implies she found satisfaction by working
on the business side of raising money for breast cancer:

I am looking to make a career change. I am currently working in the field
of education. I worked on a project this summer where I co-ordinated
and dealt with the business end of a charity ride. Two women rode
across country to raise money for breast cancer. We are looking into
how to keep the charity going???? Do you have any suggestions?

Because I am not sure what she means by all the questions marks after her question on "keep the charity going, " I answer it literally first,
providing information on fundraising sources for breast cancer. I follow this with information on fundraising as a career, providing a link
to the Foundation Center.

Congratulations on doing such important work! And, yes, I have some
suggestions. To keep the charity going????, consider writing grants.
Two excellent sources are The Feminist Majority on Breast Cancer at
http://www.feminist.org/other/bc/bchome.html/ and the Foundation
Center at http://www.fdncenter.org/. At the Foundation Center's site
you will find a wealth of information on funding provided by public, private, and corporate foundations. You'll also find info on how to write a
grant as well as job listings for people interested in professional fundraising. If you're thinking of changing career from education to something
new, you may be able to create a whole new position and lifestyle for

yourself as you raise funds for this worthwhile cause. Good luck and let me know if this information helps. Sincerely, Dr. Patricia Boer, OCC's Career Guru

One of the most common requests for information came from men and women wanting to work at home. Many wrote stating all the information on the Internet appeared to be about scams or sites that requested they send money. With few exceptions they wrote asking for resources for legitimate ways to work from home. For example, here's a very straight forward request:

I'm trying to figure out how I can make a few extra dollars at home by either using my computer or not. Have any suggestions on how to get started?

In response I wrote:

Working from home is a hot topic now! And, it often falls under the category of developing a small business. Each state has services to assist small business owners, so you might consider checking with one of the centers in your area by viewing http://www.sbaonlin.sba.gov. Another option is to search our site under Browse for Jobs by Industry. Check out the options under Telecommuting and Consulting. Or you could check Home Office, a computing magazine for small home based business ideas at http://www.smalloffice.com. Also, try New Ways to Work at http://www.nww.org/. Let me know if it helps.

Many wrote too asking for help understanding ageism in the workplace. Here a divorced 58-year-old man who wrote:

What's a guy to do? At 58, divorced in 1997, divested of my interest in a successful life and health insurance and financial advisory practice in the process and not at all ready, willing or able to retire in the traditional sense, I find myself confronted with a marketplace that values youth and technology and devalues experience when at comes with advanced years (from the point of view of the recruiter, not mine). I am a very capable salesperson, executive, coach, team builder and all around good guy but can't seem to uncover a single situation where my years of experience, accumulated skill and concomitant wisdom are of any use or value. Your advice is greatly appreciated.

Here's my reply. Because he sounds down or some might characterize as negative, I want to affirm his perceptions before offering options.
I also want to point out his skills and how these might transfer to another field. I wrote the following:

> In many ways you are right, the marketplace appears to value youth ...
> theirs is a smaller price tag unlike those of us with considerable experi-
> ence and expertise. Sometimes, it's strictly a question of dollars. How-
> ever, many small businesses and nonprofits value maturity and
> experience. Given the skills you describe (sales, executive, coach, team
> builder) why not consider a new career, one calling for these, such as a
> development officer in professional fundraising. This field particularly val-
> ues experience and maturity. Many universities, hospitals, and nonprofits
> hire fundraisers and reward them financially. To learn more about fund-
> raising, foundations, and positions in the field, check the Foundation
> Center at http://www.fdn.org/. Also, you might look at Philanthropy
> On-line. This site links to other nonprofit jobs. Visit at
> http://www.jobs.pj.org/. Let me know if this helps.

He writes back almost immediately, saying:

> Thanks for your reply. The "jobs.pj.org" page is loaded with good "stuff"
> that will most certainly help. The "fdn.org" address points to a French
> home page that does not seem to address the subject at hand. Is there
> something I'm missing? Thanks in advance.

Yes! He's right, there is definitely something missing. This happened rarely but it can and does happen. It's one of the possible barriers to communication online. The best information may be lost due to
a misspelled word or address (URL) that is out of date. Fortunately, he
wrote back. His message shows his appreciation and interest in receiving the correct address. In this case it was an easy mistake to fix, I had
simply mistyped the address leaving out a word. Here's the correct
URL for the Foundation Center http://www.fdncenter.org.

COMMUNITY INFORMATION AND REFERRALS

Just as identifying and searching for appropriate online information
starts with the basics, searching for community resources starts there,

too. It starts with hard copy community directories and agencies that counselors make available to in-person clients.

Human Services Agencies

For example, most communities have a comprehensive directory of human services. In Indianapolis, it's called the Rainbow Book, listing more than 800 community agencies and programs. This single publication provides information to serve the gay and lesbian community, ex-offenders, people with disabilities, new immigrants, the unemployed as well as resources for dealing with everything from bankruptcy to bereavement, attorney referrals, caregiver services as well as how to file complaints, earn a GED, or deal with learning disabilities. Now online, this publication is available via the Internet at http://www.irni.org/links.html. On this site are links to the main office of United Way, another excellent community resource with additional links on volunteer opportunities at http://www.uwci.org/links.html. Direct links are also provided to nonprofit organizations in the community. Most communities have something similar. If not, a search can be conducted through a national directory of United Way agencies at http://www.unitedway.org or through the public library.

Public Libraries

Today, public libraries are considered information centers. Most are linked together through a vast network of additional links leading straight to the library of congress. For example I can start in Marion County where I live at http://www.imcpl.lib.in.us and link from there to any state. All I need do is either follow the links on the library Web page or substitute the "in" in the URL for the two-letter abbreviation for any state of interest. Interestingly, sometimes the oldest and most obvious resources are often the best, meaning, the public library can be the best place to start.

Resources on Your Desk

And don't over look the wealth of resources that float across your desk. *Working Woman Magazine* (1999) published a special Internet issue, at http://www.workingwoman.com. The issue offers a 25-page guide of the best Web sites for women in 25 categories from books, career moves, and health to purchasing computers, distance learning opportunities, investing, and parenting. For distance education UCLA heads the list at http://www.onlinelearning.net followed by Colorado State for those interested in an online MBA at http://www.biz.colostate.edu/mba/distance/distance.htm. Donna Hoffman, professor of management and co-founder in 1994 of Vanderbilt University's Project 2000, is quoted as worrying about the "creation of a disadvantaged class of non-Net user," adding that "if you're not online, you're not in society." Her concerns stem from what she calls the race divide, noting that even as the prices of computers decline, lower income Blacks are lagging in terms of computer ownership compared with Whites. Although she doesn't offer solutions, she raises some important questions.

SUMMARY

One might think providing information and referral a simple task, and sometimes it is. However, to provide the right information and the most appropriate for an individual client is a skill in itself, complicated by the shear volume of online information. Counselors can start by trusting what they already know and drawing on their experiences from in-person practice. Professional organizations, community agencies, and directories like *Working Woman's Special Internet Issue* are resources not to overlook. Equally important are the number of online college career centers as well as online commercial career centers like Monster.com. And, least counselors get lost in the maze of information overload, we can look to our public libraries and those at our alma maters for assistance, remembering what's good for our clients is good for us too.

DISCUSSION QUESTIONS

1. Define and discuss how a counselor provides appropriate information and referrals.
2. Do you agree with the concept, "you don't have to over answer." Give an example and explain why you agree or disagree.
3. Name three sources to help you get started with an online career search. Explain your choices and why you think they are of value.
4. What are two common resources many counselors overlook?
5. Are there other resources, not mentioned, that you would recommend adding?

PART

Preparing for a Paradigm Shift

Starting with chapter 8, Embracing Technology, this section of the book looks to the future of online services. Examples of messages that were returned due to computer glitches or technology failures, demonstrate the barriers or the downside of this medium. The chapter also discusses the importance of support for putting a human face on technology in the delivery of career counseling services. Closely related is chapter 9, Encouraging Qualitative Research, or what professionals can learn from reviewing and reflecting on qualitative studies. An analysis from interactive research methodologies offers suggestions for counselor training, supervision, and the development of practice models. Chapter 10, Emerging Practice Models, offers a summary of key reflections on 11 lessons from the road with suggestions for a practice that reinforces the purpose of the book, valuing online career services as the medium for the 21st century. these last three chapters offer insights for researchers and practitioners alike as we move forward to fulfill the NCDA mission "to facilitate the career development of all people across the life span."

8

Embracing Technology

When former ACA President Donna Ford took office, she was quoted as saying that she was looking forward to viewing the future in a different way. She chose as her theme "Formatting Our Future," selecting the term *format* to emphasize the need for counselors to take a lead in the delivery of counseling services via the Internet, Ford (1999) stated:

> It is better to embrace the new technology, learn all we can, get over our personal fears and decide how to provide ethical, competent counseling services for the public. As counselors we are in the position to set the standards that will guide the future. (p. 5)

Ford's presidential theme reflects attention to the third issue in the debate about online counseling technology. Debaters ask what impact technology has on the counseling process in both keeping up with its changes and its failures. Like many counselors, my journey to embrace technology was gradual and in many ways skeptical. Not only did I worry about technology's changes, I worried that technology was yet another way for business to take over our field.

While thinking I was so savvy, I often denied technology's impact. For example, working with clients in individual sessions or workshop settings, I would say, "all fields cycle." Before the days of full employment, most clients knew exactly what this meant. They could picture a friend or relative who left a field like real estate. When interest rates soared, causing the market to drop they knew of agents who quit. Or, they would remember an unemployed or aspiring teacher changing careers when the field was flooded. Or, they could even recall what happened to nurses when managed care entered the scene. Some had their own horror stories to share about their experiences, which is why they were seeking direction through my services.

Secure in the belief that transitions increase the demand for career counselors, I glossed over the impact that technology was making in my own field. I missed some beginning signals. Later, discovering search engines to identify college or company information for clients, the impact was more apparent as I observed Web pages appearing or disappearing overnight.

Suddenly, it seemed that a career counselor needed to be a cross between a librarian, a researcher, and a computer guru. With more and more information available on the Web, it appeared that technology threatened to replace the field, as practitioners folded offices or merged into different fields. Clients, too, expressed frustration in trying to identify appropriate online information and the value of posting resumes online.

Today, online users hardly realize that career services via the Web are still in its infancy, less than the age of a preschooler. As daily changes continue to occur, I know what I write today may be outdated when this volume goes to press. Still, I believe it is important to chronicle the evolution of events and services. Because, just as the Internet is changing the way career counselors conduct practice, the changes challenge us to expand our knowledge base and develop best practices.

To respond to the challenges, Tyler (cited in Morrissey, 1997), an assistant professor of counselor education at Florida Gulf Coast University, called for "differentiation between counseling, education, crisis intervention and other services that could be performed via the Internet" (p. 4).

OTHER ELECTRONIC CAREER INTERVENTIONS

A closer look at definitions on electronic career services helps to distinguish online career counseling from other online career interventions, including crisis interventions.

- **Usenet newsgroups:** These are discussion groups, known as Usenet, or online groups in which individuals discuss a topic through text messages posted in a public discussion area. It allows readers to reach as many as 100 e-mail messages/senders in a short time. The flip side is that the message/discussion is public. Usenet newsgroups also are known as bulletin boards and message boards, or places on the net where one can read, leave, and respond to messages pertaining to a selected topic.

- **Web forums:** Web forums are like Usenet, except these exist only on the Web. According to Dixon (1998), Web forums are less inhabited than Usenets and therefore users have an easier time getting to know a handful of people who frequent the forum.

- **Listservs/mailing lists:** These are discussion groups carried on by e-mail. They may be either public (i.e., archived or stored on the Usenet) or private lists.

- **Message Boards:** Message boards work like an old-fashion bulletin board, where individuals can post messages or advertise something with someone designated to monitor the board. Online message boards are set up by topic areas, often called "Ask the Experts" or defined by a specific topical category like the 24 topics listed on Monster.com at http://community.monster.com/ #boardlist. Experts range in backgrounds from NCCC to employment attorneys, from resume specialists to specialists in self-employment, careers for Latinos, and aging in the workplace.

- **Toolkits:** Monster.com has also introduced the idea of "toolkits" on special topics or directed at special populations like women, older workers, those in military transition, career changers, and those with nonprofit careers. Toolkits provide specialized information on these topics as well as links to message boards, resources, and books. The career changers' toolkit offers two unique features: assessment links at http://content.monster.com/tools/personality/links.html, and multiple ways to research an employer and/or industry at http://campus.monster.com/links/research.

- **Chats:** Online chats or chat rooms are Web pages, that allow users to type a message to a group of people in real time, that is, users do not have to wait for responses to messages to arrive later. They simply type their message, press "enter," and the message appears on the screen (in a communal chat area) for others to read and make replies. According to Dixon (1998), "chat rooms tend toward quippy conversations as opposed to substantive conversations" (p.168).

- **Video and teleconferencing:** According to Sussman (1998), real-time video, audio, and teleconferencing has not arrived to counseling. It is in the near future, meaning, 2 to 4 years, and holds the promise of making online counseling, "the next best thing to being there."

E-MAIL CAREER COUNSELING

In contrast to the public electronic interventions just outlined, I define career counseling over the Internet as:

> Individualized e-mail career counseling, a specialty of WebCounseling, integrating professional career counseling and career planning services and utilizing electronic resources to communicate and deliver services when the client and the counselor are in separate or remote locations.

What are popularly known as chats, message boards, listserves, or other group activities, sometimes called online career counseling, are excluded from this definition. By definition, these activities are conversational in nature, similar to the advisement models used by teachers, librarians, or professional expertise offered via talk radio, television interviews, or newspaper columns.

One-to-One Basis

Like telephone counseling, a one-to-one basis implies a deeper level of involvement with the client. This means my definition of online career counseling is confined to e-mail career counseling practiced on an individualized, one-to-one basis, with the e-mail messages and responses written between the client and the career counselor within a specified time frame, similar to individual appointments. The process involves a total-person approach similar to that described by Crites (1981). E-mail career counseling is an integration model involving both career counseling modalities and career planning services, including information and referrals or links to services specific to client questions, and with an appreciation for the client's context and worldviews.

LESSON 9: EMBRACING TECHNOLOGY IS RELATED TO SUPPORT

So how did I embrace technology, becoming an advocate for online career counseling? How did my role change from providing in-person career counseling to using an online format? Some might say I was in the right place at the right time. True. Yet I also believe it was a natural evolution, one resulting from a growing interest in technology coupled with support to pursue my interests from the OCC.

MY PROCESS TO EMBRACE TECHNOLOGY

Although I often ignored technology's impact, I did keep abreast of changes reported in the literature and at professional meetings. I also used technology in daily tasks, taking classes to improve my skills. Furthermore, I was the first private practitioner in my city to offer vocational assessments online. So, when Susan Bryant, OCC's product manager, along with Craig Besant, vice president of marketing, visited me to share ideas for starting an online career magazine I was intrigued. From them I learned OCC.com was headquartered in Indianapolis where president Bill Warren, first started the company. By spring 1998, OCC was not only successful financially, it was nationally visible, dubbed by Dixon (1998) among the Big Seven of all sites and among the top five sites for job seekers.

Seeking to expand online career services for job seekers, Susan and Craig were looking for a consultant with national credentials to help launch a magazine. At the time, I didn't dream an online publication would spark such interest nor present me the ideal situation to research the online career counseling process. Not only would I have support for my contributions, I would have the confidence of the company's president. I was also to find a colleague in Susan Bryant, herself a counselor. Through Craig, I would have added support including approval for additional funding, opportunities to conduct live chats, and approval for ongoing technical support. Nor did I have a clue that my contributions to a start-up career magazine would lead to a daily love affair with this new medium as I served online clients and embraced technology to conduct practice.

Identifying My Role

Initially, my role called for me to serve as the magazine's career consultant, authoring articles and answering questions posed by the readership. Once I agreed to the arrangement, Susan's job was to suggest a format and title for the magazine as well as a series of topics for me to address. I, too, would need a title as well as a separate page on which to post my credentials.

The first title proposed was Dr. Pat to be the magazine's Career Doctor, that is, until it was discovered another site used that title for their career advisor. Then OCC's public relations department stepped in, adding a new twist. The magazine was to have a theme reflecting its title and mine. Thus, *Career Karma* was born with its Career Guru providing "career enlightenment" for readers.

Primary Concerns

At the time, posting my credentials appropriately was my chief concern. I wanted to be sure OCC listed my education and experience as an NCCC appropriately. This proved to be no problem as Susan and Craig were in agreement that my commitment to *WebCounseling Standards* was an asset and they were more than happy to provide links to both the NBCC and NCDA.

Because I saw my role as one of a consultant to OCC.com, I didn't give much thought to providing counseling via the Internet. Rather, I viewed my role as similar to the work I contributed to columns in the *Indianapolis Business Register*.

Once the Web page was designed with my bio posted, the next step was to announce the premier issue of *Career Karma* with the Career Guru answering selective questions (four or five) to be posted publicly in the magazine. Susan planned to screen the questions, sending me a selection for consideration, simple enough, not requiring sophisticated technology. Then, 3 weeks before launch date, to everyone's surprise, more than 250 questions began arriving faster than anyone could read!

Shifting Gears

Quickly, we shifted gears. For instance, OCC technicians were called to network my office to OCC's server. This allowed all messages to be delivered via e-mail directly to my desktop, ensuring *Career Karma* questions would be separate from my personal e-mail on AOL. Although users were informed that submitting their questions meant they were agreeing to have their answers selected for public posting in the magazine or online, they were also assured that their identity would remain confidential. Neither their names nor addresses would be posted.

Once the service was announced, messages were secured in my e-mail by a secret log on and password. When the messages poured in faster than anticipated, I quickly needed to develop a method to handle the traffic, more than 30 e-mails per day. Suddenly, too, my role changed from consulting to screening and providing individualized responses to each message. In other words, OCC decided to sponsor a very unique job-seeker service. Through the magazine, job seekers could send a personal question to the Career Guru, who would answer them individually and confidentially. The announcement for the service included a disclaimer that the service is not a substitute for professional career counseling. The announcement follows:

Need some career enlightenment?

Send your career questions to our Guru, Dr. Patricia Boer. Questions that have the broadest application to many job seekers are posted here anonymously. If you have a question or concern about making a career shift, adapting to a new corporate culture, doing your best in an interview, managing workplace stress, or anything else career-related, please send to the careerguru@occ.ocm.

We look forward to hearing your questions (and please let us know how the Guru's advice has worked out for you).

Note: Although the advice from the Career Guru (Dr. Patricia Boer) is based on her extensive experience in the field of career development, the responses provided are not a substitute for professional career counseling. Readers are encouraged to pursue individual assistance from a qualified professional for more in depth answers to their career concerns. To find a qualified career counselor in your area or to learn more about the services career counselors provide, visit the National Board for Certified Counselor or the National Career Development Association for more information.

The announcement was followed by a link to information about my credentials and background. By using the services, clients realized their questions and personal responses might be chosen to be publicly yet anonymously posted. In effect, by sending a question, clients were waiving their rights to privacy. With this announcement, I was confident messages would be free of personal information. More than 850 messages would prove me wrong. As e-mails poured into my mailbox, I observed the personal nature of each and need to prioritize by issue or search online for resources, links or referrals before responding. Also, I needed to track who sent what, on which topic, which day, week or month, and which ones had been answered or returned. To help me, OCC technicians installed an e-mail software package, Eudora, allowing me to sort questions and answers into online folders categorizing them by month, thank you messages, and/or returned messages. Eudora software was invaluable in helping me track the large volume of messages.

With multiple levels of support from OCC.com, I easily embraced the medium and online services. Without support I am convinced I would not have taken the risks I did. As a private practitioner, it meant limiting my in-person practice to devote myself full time to online clients. It also meant venturing into a new medium with few practice guidelines. Support helped me take risks, move forward, and quickly become an advocate of technology. For example, not only was the company's president pleased with my work, when he learned I was renting a laptop to take on vacation, he volunteered his. And, when I needed technical support a technician was assigned to make office calls as I created and set-up a new process. Susan's support was invaluable, too. She stayed in daily contact with me either by phone or e-mail, and sometimes both. Together we designed and worked on reference lists like interviewing questions, resume tips, and other job search resources as well as selecting appropriate online assessments or developing online quizzes. It was a pleasure to work with her and have the opportunity to be as creative as I liked.

Responding to Client Questions

My early process of responding to clients included printing each question and numbering them individually. Next, I would read quickly, highlighting key words, and issues, prioritizing and reflecting on responses to write, generally within 48 hours. As stated in previous chapters common questions revolved around immigration issues, telecommuting, changing careers after a downsizing, preparing for the interview, and specifics about various fields, such as what can one do with a degree in psychology, human development, sociology, history, and/or one of the languages. Teachers and nurses, attorneys, and even doctors wrote asking how to transition into alternative careers. This meant I needed to search online for resources, learning all I could about immigration issues as well as emerging career areas. For instance, forensic nursing, nursing infomatics, legal nursing, and parish nursing are all emerging specialties within the field. Like many teachers, nurses often think leaving direct service means creating a whole new skills set. Soon, I learned that searching for customized links made answering individual questions time-consuming and called for greater efficiency on my part.

Identifying Search Engines

Finding a good search engine was the first step. Alta Vista was my search engine of choice until I discovered Snap.com. Unlike Yahoo, a directory providing more links than needed, Snap.com narrowed searches, often providing specific resources such as a professional association, article, or specialty site related to a profession. For example, Findlaw.com at http://www.findlaw.com is an excellent resource for attorneys seeking alternatives both within and outside their field.

Once I became more efficient, I began experimenting by answering online directly. Instead of printing and prioritizing questions, I began answering directly online on a first come basis. This freed my time to search more extensively when needed. Within 2 months of working 10 to 12 hour days, I developed a better system. With many resources and links literally at my fingertips, I was able to handle a much larger clientele than I thought possible.

Just as I became comfortable, believing I had found a niche, I discovered two realities about online services: online services create their own barriers, and things constantly change.

EXPERIENCING TECHNOLOGY BARRIERS

The first barrier occurred early in my online experience. It happened when replies to questions were returned with some type of error message like:

- Returned mail: User unknown
- Returned mail: Host unknown (host not found)
- Undeliverable mail: No such users
- This message could not be delivered
- Mail System Error
- Delivery Notification: Delivery has failed

Here are examples of questions received with my replies to the sender returned, stating: "Returned mail, user unknown."

Example 1: Returned Mail, User Unknown

Dear Dr. Boer,
I have been trying for several months to secure a job in northern CA. But so far, no luck. I was wondering if I'd have better luck if I bit the bullet and moved there without a job. I am currently in upstate NY. Also, is it true that I should be expecting to make 60% more than I do in Upstate NY, if I land a job in San Francisco? Thanks!

Here's my reply ...

> If you can afford to move, I'd say bite the bullet. It's always easier to find a job when you live in the locale, rather than applying long distance. Also, people are more likely to help you when you're new in town, just as they are when you're leaving.
>
> So take advantage of tapping into your network both in New York as well as California. Do as much research as you can on opportunities in San Francisco, if that's your destination. For example, each state has its own site. California's is http://www.state.ca.us/. On this site you can go to other sites listing job opportunities and salaries. Also, use the salary calculator (on our Career Services page, under Relocation) to help you answer salary differentials between your home in NY and San Francisco. Good luck and let me know how your relocation progresses.

Example 2: Returned Mail: User Unknown

Here's another example from a high school teacher wanting a portable career. Her message appears here, yet my reply was returned stating, "Returned Mail: user unknown:

> Dear Guru
> Currently, I am a high school teacher with eight years experience. I am also married to a military member. I am growing tired of changing school systems every three years and essentially restarting my career. I want to change to a field where frequent moves on my part doesn't necessarily mean that I have to find a new employer. I've thought that technical writing might be such a field but I don't know how or where to start looking. I have an MA in linguistics and am fluent in French and Spanish. What advice do you have?

Here's my response ...

> Getting started in technical communications is like getting started in any field, even teaching. It's starts with:
>
> 1. A dream or idea, generally followed by gathering information, connecting with others who are involved in the field or will help you advance. It may require gaining the necessary training or credentials. Since you have an MA in linguistics and are fluent in French and Spanish, you may be half way there already.

2. Investigation of the field. Gather as much information as you can about technical writing. Or review the basics outlined in the online book, Getting Started in Technical Communications at http://www.ace1.com/webbook.htm.
3. Professional Associations. Learn more about the field by linking to professional organizations such as the Society for Technical Communications at http://www.stc-va.org/. On this site, you'll find a database of job listings by state, salary, and permanent or contract arrangements. You'll also find information on local chapters and salary surveys.
4. Additional links. Other professional groups include the Association of Teachers of Technical Writing at http://english.ttu.edu/attw/. This site, too, offers additional resources and links you'll want to review, such as links to the Association for Business Communication and the Society for Intercultural Education, Training and Research.
5. And, because your husband is in the military, inquire at his duty station about the Armed Forces Communication and Electronics Association. This group could connect you to contract opportunities in technical writing making your relocations a win–win for both of you.

Once you get started gathering information, you'll discover the many options offered by this field and be better prepared to weigh its pros and cons for your lifestyle. Good luck and let me know if this helps.

Of course, this client was never able to let me know if my research helped her. She never received the message. Error messages, like these two examples, represented 10% of the first replies sent as we set up the system. This was very frustrating, not only because the client would not receive the message, but because it meant valuable time was lost for others who were anxiously awaiting replies delivered error free. Even the following one, a favorite of mine because it referenced my hometown was returned, host unknown.

Example 3: Returned Mail: Host Unknown

I just recently got laid off. I WAS INSTALLING ELECTRONIC WATER METER'S. I enjoyed the job but due to lack of work I was laid off. .I WAS TOLD BY some maintenance people that if I was willing to relocate to California, San Diego or somewhere out west. They were sure I could get a job. At an Avalon apartment complex. I was told they would pay for me to relocate. I'm not sure what to do. Don't sound bad. I like the beach. DO you know anything about San Diego?

My reply began ...

> If you like the beach, you'll love San Diego. I know a lot about it. San Diego is my hometown. That means I'm also very prejudiced. You must not take my word for it. You need to check it out yourself. Read all you can about San Diego in San Diego Magazine online at http://www.sandiego-online.com/. On this site, you'll be able to investigate various lifestyles, dining, entertainment, etc. Then take time to utilize the resources of OCC's relocation page at http://www.occ.com/occ/career/relocation/. On this page, you can determine or calculate salary and living cost differentials as well as other expenses related to relocation. By reading and gathering information on San Diego and similar cities in the west, you'll make the right decision for yourself. Good luck and let me know what you decide.

It is important to note that these return messages are examples of providing appropriate information and referrals versus examples of career counseling per se. Nor do they represent messages of clients in crisis. Interestingly, one question in the debate on technology's barriers asks about crisis counseling. Some ask what happens when technology fails and the client is in crisis half way around the globe? In the case of the 850 clients I served through e-mail career counseling, this was not an issue. Among the sample of error messages, not one represented a client in crisis, that is, a life or death situation. The technology failures experienced are better characterized as frustrating either for me as a provider or for the client awaiting a response. Although there is the potential for career situations to produce the need for crisis counseling and intervention, this was not indicated during my 5 months of online practice.

OTHER COMPUTER PROBLEMS

In addition to the returned messages, other glitches happened periodically like getting bumped off the OCC server while I composed online responses. Susan referred this to one of the technicians, sending me the following reply. Her message is an example of server problems. When OCC's server experienced technical problems, there was a ripple effect in my office. For instance, Susan writes about a problem with the NBCC link on my bio page:

> Hi Pat,
> Just wanted to let you know that the Career Karma link isn't working

yet. So, someone cannot get to the NBCC link by clicking on it. You may need to add the NBCC link in your messages for now.

Also, Trever e-mailed me back and said the following:
"She can probably solve her "getting bumped off" problem (if she leaves Eudora running all the time) just by going into (in Eudora) Tools, then Options, then Checking Mail, and making certain that the time interval for checking new messages is set to something less than 15 minutes. (Five minutes is good.)"

Susan was excellent at keeping me informed, not to mention assisting me. She was encouraging and supportive of my work, ever affirming and keeping me posted on events at OCC as well. Here's an example of one of the e-mails she sent that demonstrates other technical barriers as well as her own affirming style. In the message, she sends me a disclaimer that she wants to post reference the Self Directed Search. She writes:

Hi Pat:
Here's what I have, let me know what you think: The self-assessment inventories provided by Online Career Center are intended as one of many career resources available to our users. Although our inventories have been carefully selected to provide the greatest benefit to the user, there are limits to the type of information online self-assessment can provide. Readers are encouraged to pursue individual assistance from a qualified professional for more in-depth interpretation and answers to their career questions. To learn more about the services career counselors provide, or to find a counselor in your area, visit the National Board of Certified Counselors or the National Career Development Association for more information.

I think that by saying there are limits to the type of info self assessment can provide, we are basically saying we cannot guarantee your results. We could run this by our lawyer, too I guess to see if he feels its necessary we explicitly state we are not endorsing or guaranteeing results. I just don't want to give the inadvertent impression to users that we are not confident in our tests. –Susan

And, here's an example of how she kept me posted on upcoming changes at OCC. For example, when Netscape heard what we were doing, a new alliance was formed between the sites. Susan sent this message:

Hi Pat!
I don't want to freak you out, but the Guru may be getting a much bigger audience soon!! Craig and Emma Frimann (our VP Alliance person) are trying to work out a deal with Netscape/Netcenter to be a part of their Career Center. Guess what part of our OCC content they want to put there?? "Words of Wisdom from the Career Guru" of course! Here's the page on Netscape:
http://home.netscape.com/netcenter/careercenter/index.html?cp= hom09cbca. This deal is all speculation now, but I thought I would fill you in case it does develop. Are you ready to be on Netscape???!!! Wow! Pat Boer- "Career Guru to the Universe!!!"

And, later, after the deal was made, Susan sent these updates:

Hi Pat!
We're live on Netcenter! A new question will appear daily.
http://occ.netscape.com/careerguru/

Hi Pat!
Guess what?! The Career Guru on Netscenter got 1,024 hits yesterday! About 1/3 clicked on "more questions from the guru" at the bottom of the page that took them to Career Karma magazine. Yay! these are good stats!! -Susan

And, still later, she sent this:

Pat, you're answers to guru questions are GREAT! I just got done reading through all of them. You really do a super job. I'm so lucky I found you!!! I have to pick the rest of the month's Q's to go online with Netscape today/tomorrow so I'll try to send a copy over to you prior. THANKS AGAIN PAT!

When you are trying something new for the first time, it's empowering to have respect and support from those who have hired you. To have someone there daily, cheering you on, is an extra plus. Suddenly, 12 hours days are shorter. Acknowledgment makes a difference, too, when inevitable changes and new challenges occur.

ONLINE COMMERCIAL CAREER CENTERS CONSTANTLY CHANGE

Continuing change at online career centers reflect the nature of the online industry. One way to observe changes is among shifts in its personnel, which happen regularly. Personnel move in and out of their roles either as a result of a promotion, better opportunity at another site, or company mergers. In the case of OCC, all three occurred.

By mid-October, Susan sent me another message announcing OCC, and the StudentCenter.com were expecting to merge with MonsterBoard effective January 1999. The three sites planned to pool resources under the umbrella title, Monster.com. This is why clicking on OCC.com or Student Center.com, now links you to Monster.com. What this merger eventually meant in Indianapolis was a retirement for OCC's founder and president, Bill Warren, and promotions for both Susan and Craig, with Craig moving to new headquarters in Maynard, Massachusetts.

These changes signaled the end of my contract with OCC. When Monster extended an offer for me to join their career experts to moderate a message board and conduct live chats I accepted. Although, not online career counseling, working with Monster was an opportunity to continue utilizing my online career services skills.

THE HUMAN FACE OF TECHNOLOGY

After my work with OCC.com ended, I felt a loss. OCC.com had been a unique experience both to embrace technology and to pursue online practice. It was also unique because the company supported my efforts on three levels, all levels necessary for success on any job.

1. Financial support: This helped me in two ways. It freed my time exclusively for online practice and allowed me to hire my colleague, Dena Weinstein, to oversee my private practice during the duration of the project.
2. Leadership support: With OCC's endorsement from president Bill Warren to Craig Besant and Susan Bryant, I felt empowered to take risks and embrace technology.
3. Technical support: Trever Furnish and the OCC technical team answered questions on the spot, making my online life easier.

Reflecting on my process to embrace technology and the support I received from OCC, coupled with client voices, reinforced three other conclusions drawn earlier about this medium.

Three Conclusions

As suggested in earlier chapters, I propose three points regarding career counseling online. Online career counseling is:

1. Personal counseling: It is personal counseling because it is difficult if not impossible to separate personal issues from career information,
2. Similar to in-person counseling: It requires counselors to follow the same codes of ethics and standards of practice including counselor skills, attitudes, knowledge, and respect for various worldviews.
3. A Specialty of WebCounseling: As a specialty of WebCounseling, a new career counseling credential would replace the retired NBCC career specialty, thereby distinguishing who is qualified to practice career counseling and who offers something different.

And, further reflections on who is qualified to practice career counseling online and who offers something different lead to lesson 10, that is, the need for a new credential for online career counseling practice.

LESSON 10: DEVELOPING NEW CREDENTIALS FOR ONLINE PRACTICE

The establishment of a new credential for the practice of online career counseling is not only driven by my reflections on practice, it is driven by society's growing reliance on technology. A new credential addresses the need to embrace technology and provides a vehicle to protect public interest. Client voices demonstrate that credentials serve as a vehicle to identify qualified career counselors over the Internet. As reported in chapter 3, clients consistently wrote, saying things like, "I've been looking for a nationally certified career counselor." My credentials indicated I could help them and they could trust me. Counselor credentials were mentioned more often and appeared more important to clients than issues of privacy and confidentiality.

By posting my credentials online as an NCCC online, certified by the NBCC, clients were able to link to the ethical standards I follow for providing career counseling over the Internet. These links offered consumer guidelines for selecting a career counselor as well as client rights and responsibilities. Thus, clients were able to determine initially what services are provided, who they are for, and about my credentials.

With the retirement of the NBCC National Certified Career Counselor specialty in June 1999, the practice of online career counseling has no way for clients to distinguish it from other services like career coaching. A new credential would specify for clients and counselors alike a reliable way to distinguish which individuals are qualified to provide online career counseling from others offering something different, such as coaching or advising. This 10th of my 11 lessons is also in keeping with directives from Ford (1999), who emphasized the need for counselors to take the lead in the delivery of counseling services via the Internet.

SUMMARY

To embrace technology takes many forms. For me it meant a gradual transformation until a human face accelerated the process, that is, working with key individuals within the OCC community. It was not a computer course, nor the latest in technologies in the OCC arsenal that led me to embrace technology, it was the human face of doing business with outstanding individuals who supported and encouraged my work. It was also the human face of the clients who responded with appreciation for the benefits received through this service. Technology is a tool, and like any tool it needs fine tuning and constant care to keep running. What made the challenges attractive were the faces of its people. By going online to practice career counseling and dealing with the glitches mentioned, whether those involving return messages or server problems, I learned it is a human face that makes or breaks this powerful medium. A new credential for online practice is one way to improve the human face of this medium. A new credential will recognize counselor online expertise providing guidance and support for counselors to embrace technology.

Although I fully recognize that counselors need training in technology and need to learn all they can to implement online services, I am equally aware that without support new hardware and training opportunities will not be the answer. What I have learned on this journey is that if you are venturing into new territory, if you are looking to embrace technology, when there is support, you will. It's that simple. Whether you are in the business community, government, private practice, or the academic world, with support you will develop plans to learn technology, keep up with changes in the ethical codes, and take risks to implement services globally. Without support you are likely to label technology a barrier instead of tool for the advancement of client transformation. ACA's new president, Ford (1999) clearly recognized this when she selected her theme, "Formatting Our Future," extending her support for counselors to embrace technology.

DISCUSSION QUESTIONS

1. What is the definition of *online career counseling*? Do you agree with this definition? Why or Why not? Describe at least other three online career interventions and how these are different from or the same as online career counseling

2. Name some of the typical online line computer problems a counselor is likely to face conducting career counseling over the Internet? What is meant by the phrase, "Putting a human face on technology"? Do you agree with this concept? Why or Why not?

3. What do you believe influences counselor to embrace or not embrace technology? Give examples.

4. What is driving the need for a new credential and is a new credential necessary for the practice of online career counseling? Give examples and reasons to support your position.

9

Encouraging Qualitative Research

Although perspectives differ regarding the WebCounseling debate, there is agreement about the need for research. Research is the fourth issue in the debate on WebCounseling. Leaders and counselors alike ask: "How do we know if WebCounseling is helpful or harmful? What are best practice models for online career counseling?" These same professionals call for increased efforts for research. In the NCDA Annual Review: Practice and Research in Career Counseling, Niles (1997), reviewing practice and research in career counseling and development stated: "the proliferation of online career services ... requires researchers and practitioners to increase their efforts aimed at translating career theory into effective and innovative career interventions" (pp. 134–135). Two years later in the same publication, Young and Chen (1999) noted, "increased attention to qualitative based assessment would enhance the field" (p. 127). Tyler (cited in Morrissey, 1997), an assistant professor of counselor education at Florida Gulf Coast University, called for the importance of "differentiation between counseling, education, crisis intervention and other services that could be performed via the Internet" (p. 4).

Not only must we differentiate between terms, we need qualitative studies to inform us on several aspects of career counseling. We need studies to identify and describe client populations and issues. We need descriptive research to identify appropriate interventions and resources for global populations. Descriptive studies will inform us, too, about counselor characteristics and gaps in counselor training to better prepare online counselors to address online client issues. Qualitative research, particularly studies addressing the voices of both clients and counselors will provide insights and guidance about proceeding in this new practice medium.

Qualitative studies reflect what Paisely (1997) described as the importance of personalizing our history:

> The personal component adds the texture we might otherwise ignore. As counseling comes of age as a discipline and as we as counselors acknowledge the diversity of our experience as well as our different ways of knowing, we must also come to a place where we can honor both empirical data and the power of personal narrative. To limit ourselves professionally to one approach also limits our definition of who we are and who we can become. (p.4)

METHODOLOGY FOR ONLINE PRACTICE

Aware that little research on career counseling over the Internet is available, I chose a qualitative study with interactive research methods. As noted earlier, Merriam and Simpson (1989) defined interactive research methods as having three distinguishing characteristics from other forms of social science research:

1. The researcher serves as a facilitator for problem solving ... (and) ... as a catalyst between the research findings and those individuals most likely to benefit or take action from the findings.
2. The results of research are intended for immediate application by those engaged in the research or by those for whom the research was initiated.
3. The design of interactive research is formulated while the research is in progress, rather than being totally predetermined at the outset of the study.

These characteristics match what I perceived as a work in progress, that is, I served as both the facilitator and researcher for online career counseling; the results were intended for immediate use and for the benefit of the client users; and, the research was formulated during the study rather than, "being totally predetermined at the outset of the study." Consequently, from client messages received I made observations about client populations and issues, recording these in journal notes. By tracking the messages and categorizing them into online folders, I identified resources helpful to clients, further identifying representative samples of common questions and responses from a population of 850 clients. Like the autobiography, client messages serve as an important qualitative method. Lancy (1993) cited to Langness and Frank (1981) to remind us how we can "record the direct testimony of those rare individuals who are able to provide us with a vivid picture of life in realms otherwise closed to us outsiders" (p. 5).

USING A FOURFOLD STRATEGY

To provide a vivid picture of online career counseling, my methodology or strategy for procedures was fourfold:

1. Understanding of the role of instrumentation in qualitative research.
2. Collecting data.
3. Analyzing the data.
4. Conducting an ongoing review of the literature to support observations and data analysis.

The role of instrumentation in qualitative research means the instrument is the researcher. This means that as a researcher I must be a skilled questioner, as well as a skilled observer, and an insightful analyst. Because I have conducted previous studies in ethnographic research methods and taught master's level graduate students qualitative methodology for the Department of Educational Leadership at Ball State University, these methods are familiar and come naturally to me.

My second strategy involved collecting evidence or my observations about the online processes, which were carefully recorded in journal notes. In addition, it meant tracking representative client messages to illustrate specific observations and reflections from this online practice. My third strategy was data analysis. I read and re-read journal notes and representative samples of client messages. An analysis conducted was similar to the method Lancy (1993) suggested in the work of Lauer and Asher (1988, cited in Lang, 1993):

> Sometimes the task is called coding—the setting up and labeling of categories, which then become the variables of the study ... the broader term for this effort is content analysis, which is a major measurement procedure.... The method is designed for use with communication data of all kinds: ... letters, and so forth. (p. 26)

In addition, ongoing reviews of the literature (Strategy 4) added to my reflections, confirming variables or lessons learned. For instance, to support my findings on anonymity (that anonymity increases access), the literature indicated a similar observation by Haas (2000). Haas noted "Another benefit for clients is the increased sense of being anonymous" (p. 26). Further Haas, pointing to Garry Walz (in press), co-author of *Cybercounseling and Cyberlearning: Strategies and Resources for the Millennium*, (in press) appeared to confirm other conclusions such as "online counseling can be more than giving advice and has the ability to be therapeutic." Literature drawing attention to the need to clarify terms, utilize disclaimers, and make clients aware of the limitations of online services are additional verifications of my observations or lessons related to the ethical practice of online career counseling. This literature is also consistent with my observation that safeguarding the online counselor–client relationship is similar to or the same as safeguarding the relationship in person.

THE FINDINGS

An analysis of observations from journal notes and representative samples of client messages resulted in 11 categories or lessons from the road. Drawn from 850 messages received at the OCC between August 1998 and January 1999, these lessons determined the importance of:

1. Valuing written texts
2. Understanding the power of anonymity
3. Viewing career counseling as personal counseling
4. Listening to client voices
5. Bridging cultural differences
6. Setting online boundaries
7. Affirming clients through assessments
8. Providing online information and referrals
9. Embracing technology
10. Developing new credentials
11. Recognizing the counselor as curriculum.

In addition, an ongoing review of the literature was used to support this analysis.

Observations From Journal Notes

As I read and reviewed my journal notes as well as responses to early questions from online clients, I noticed some of my early observations apply to current experience such as notes regarding client populations and issues.

Client Populations. Client populations included the following:

- Many foreign nationals requesting tips on immigration issues and/or the names of companies and recruiters seeking to sponsor foreign nationals.
- Many men and women wanting to work at home.
- Young college students apparently unaware of university career services.
- Family members or friends asking how to help a family member or friend.
- High numbers of career changes as the result of downsizing, unemployment, or women re-entering the workforce.
- All groups demonstrating high levels of educational attainment with BA/BS degrees or higher.

Client Issues. These issues included the following:

- Direction. Whether clients are starting out at 21 or starting over at 50, a vast majority continue to ask for help with direction, that is, "How do I get started?" or "Where do I begin?"
- Immigration. Foreign nationals represent one in ten messages. They ask primarily for information about sponsorship, visas, and in some cases directions.
- Appreciation. Next to messages about immigration issues, the next largest category of messages are thank you notes, ranging from 7% to 10%. These e-mail messages reveal that the service is helpful and that we are doing something right.
- Career change. One theme that crosses all issues and spurs many questions is the process of career change.
- Work/Family. Women still ask the majority of work/family questions. However, a growing number of men ask similar questions, particularly question about working at home.

- Advancement. Many questions revolved around continuing education, whether for a graduate degree or for some type of computer certification. Many inquire about the value of an MBA and growing numbers ask about the value of distance education and whether an employer will recognize it.
- Interviews. Everyday, there are questions about the interview process, whether they are about appropriate questions for employers to ask or how to respond to difficult questions. Many ask about telephone interviews and how to best prepare.
- Resume critiques. Like interview questions, many users attach their resumes for the counselor to critique. This could and should be a separate service by itself.
- Aging and Discrimination. Men as well as women write questions about age discrimination and it appears the questions come from younger users, that is, those in their early 40s. Several questions in this category related to downsizing, company takeovers, and buyouts.

General Reflections on Practice

As I reviewed my journal notes and read representative client messages, I noticed other themes, such as values. Regardless of the clients' presenting issues, two work values appeared throughout the messages. One related to combining or balancing work and family or personal life. Men as well as women appeared to place a high value on finding balance as evidenced by the increasing numbers of requests from both genders regarding work-at-home opportunities or how to start a home business. Also, a very high percentage of online users appeared highly educated, that is, a majority held bachelor degrees or higher. As an educated and privileged group, they often inquired about continuing education to reach their goals. Related perhaps to education was the second work value recorded, identifying meaningful work. Among career changers, the search for meaningful work appeared as a prime motivator. Representative of this group were teachers, nurses, attorneys, MBAs, and PhDs. Several were engineers, with a smaller proportion representing sales. Other indicators of values related to meaning were expressed by phrases such as "an opportunity to make a difference," "to be creative," "earn respect and/or achieve personal or professional growth."

Other Observations

In my journal, I noted other observations such as my own interest in this work springing from a desire to provide greater access to clients and the need to use reflection when responding to clients. Reflection is needed to frame and respond to written texts similarly to the type of reflection writers use to illuminate their work. Reflection is also an essential skill to utilize or understand a diverse population as well as the context of their lives. Furthermore, I noted that credentials help to build trust with clients online. Also, confidentiality did not appear to be as important to the client as emphasized in the literature. For instance, clients provided unsolicited personal information without any sign or expressed concern for breeches in confidentiality. Wanting to encourage client questions, few guidelines were provided to them explaining what was or was not appropriate to ask. Later, as more personal questions arrived or presented complex issues, I noted the need to clarify boundaries and limits for online practice.

Specific Observations.   There were two specific observations, noted in my journal:

1. The NCDA definition of "career planning services" as limited to a specific need like help with a resume was not characteristic of the numerous personal questions submitted, meaning that clients revealed in detail, personal circumstances regarding their situation.
   - More clarification is needed about career planning services. Are these to be interactive or intended as a referral service in which the vast majority of clients are to be referred to a counselor in their location?
   - Clients may want more than information, that is, they want an opportunity to vent their feelings or seek support in difficult times.
2. Online career counseling counselors first and foremost need to be effective in-person counselors meaning they are:
   - Grounded in a philosophy of career counseling theory and practice
   - Grounded in an attitude of positive regard for a diverse clientele with an understanding and acceptance of differing values and worldviews.

- Experienced with diverse populations, possessing strong counselor skills and a willingness to seek supervision when needed as well as desire for continuing education for improvement and growth.

Reflections on Learning

Once the messages poured in faster than I could keep up, I stopped journaling for a while. Consequently, I address what I learned from two aspects. First, I discuss learnings from early practice, followed by current reflections about the intervening and current months.

Early Reflections on Practice

1. The service is needed. Client voices in overwhelming numbers (250 to 300 per month) make it clear that, online career services are utilized by a large international population of adults. The overwhelming response to the *CareerKarma* magazine, and Career Guru column give direct evidence to me and to the professionals at OCC.com that the service is in demand.
2. Individuals are grateful for services. Large numbers of users of online career services write thank you notes, one in seven expressed appreciation for the services received.
3. A large population of international clients suggests that specific interventions need to be created to address their needs for immigration information and resources.
4. Online career counseling requires additional skills than in-person counseling, that is, it requires knowledge of both counseling skills and content skills such as international labor market information and the ability to write concisely.
5. Online career counseling also requires a strong comfort level working online and keeping up with the latest technology.
6. Appropriate technology (hardware) and proficiency with software makes the job easier.
7. Someone to assist in editing messages and material would free the counselor to sort through and prioritize messages more efficiently.
8. Prior career counseling experience with diverse populations seems essential to be effective at online practice.
9. Online career counseling should be a specialty in its own right.

Current Reflections on Practice

Of the nine notations first outlined from early learnings on practice via the Internet, many still hold, whereas others related to editing via technology are not as important. In particular and foremost, I believe the service is needed and should be a designated specialty of WebCounseling. A designated specialty to replace the retired NBCC Career Counseling Specialty in many ways summarizes the outcomes of this study, both those just outlined and the 11 lessons on the road. Current reflections lead me to believe that creating a new specialty serves three general needs:

1. A new online career counseling credential demonstrates counselors are taking the lead in the delivery of online career counseling.
2. A new credential will trigger new training programs to bridge gaps in current counselor preparation and continuing education.
3. A new specialty serves to prepare counselors for a paradigm shift in the delivery of career counseling services to global populations.

Trusting Clients' Views

Client voices also support the need for new credentials. Throughout the period, client messages expressed the importance placed on my credentials, demonstrating they offered clients a method to trust my ability to provide services. Messages often began with, "I read your credentials," "I've been looking for someone with your background," or "Can you suggest a counselor in my area with credentials like yours?" These messages indicate that clients look for a career counselor with credentials. This is consistent with the educational attainment level of online clients. A large majority hold post baccalaureate degrees undoubtedly influencing them to both respect the interplay and importance of credentials (theory and practice) as well as wanting someone to address their needs who holds equivalent educational attainment.

RECOMMENDATIONS FROM THE FINDINGS

Three major recommendations stand out from the findings, including: (a) clients want, use, and seek career counseling over the Internet from qualified career counselors with credentials; (b) a new career counseling credential should be established to replace the NBCC Career Specialty Credential retired in June 1999; and (c) career counseling training programs should be developed based on the counselor as curriculum.

Recommendation 1

Just as it is important for professionals to listen to our clients in individual sessions, it is equally important to listen to what they have to say in qualitative studies. The findings of this study indicate that the sheer numbers of clients seeking services are an indicator that the services are wanted and used. Client messages in written texts, particularly introductory and thank you messages, indicate counselor credentials are recommended as a key strategy in building trust between client and counselor interaction over the Internet.

Recommendation 2

The literature is replete with calls for research to clarify terminology and distinguish career counseling from career coaching and other services via the Web. Creating a new credential, a specialty of WebCounseling, to replace the NBCC Career Credential retired in June 1999, is recommended as the best way to distinguish for counselors and clients a reliable way to identify who is qualified to provide career counseling online and who is offering something different, such as coaching or advising.

Recommendation 3

Career counseling training programs to prepare counselors to provide career counseling via the Internet are recommended and should be based on the concept of the counselor as the curriculum. This recommendation grows from the other two and is elaborated on in the following section on additional support in literature.

ADDITIONAL SUPPORT IN THE LITERATURE

Clarifying Terms

The literature suggests there is a need to clarify terms and services. Pointing to Walz (in press), coauthor of *Cybercounseling and Cyberlearning: Strategies and Resources for the Millennium*, Haas (2000) noted "online counseling can be more than giving advice and has the ability to be therapeutic" (cited in Haas, 2000). Haas emphasized that the difference between talking with a counselor versus other professionals by quoting from Walz who stated: "counselors know what questions to ask that guide self-evaluation that brings insight to people" (p. 26).

Ruiz and Lipford-Sanders (1999) also emphasized the importance of differentiating between the two, noting that coaching and advice require "no specific training, experience or credentials." The authors also expressed concern about consumers being able to differentiate between the two asking, if a "counselor presents their counseling credentials and offers coaching or advice giving as separate services," then what? "What are the legal and ethical consequences of such a scenario?" Although Ruiz and Lipford-Sanders, as well as Hass are addressing counseling in general, their points easily apply to individual career counseling via e-mail. They ask important questions that a new specialty will address. By clarifying what is and is not career counseling, a more reliable high-quality service could be provided to online clients.

Training or Supervising Advantages

A new credential will spark the development of specialized training and supervision programs to assist online counselors both now and in the future as we continue to address the complex issues presented by global online populations. Course content will need to emphasize the special needs of diverse populations, with special attention to cultural differences, the special needs of women and minorities as well as people with disabilities. Our ethical codes, standards for practice and career counseling competencies, provide the framework for coursework. However, as we move forward to design new programs, it is important that we not emphasize skill over art, lest we forget our roots as counselors and the main ingredient for successful career counseling outcomes, that is, the counselor–client relationship. Stoltz-Loike (1996) reminded us:

> The counselor's respect for the client's perspective dramatically affects the success of counseling sessions ... successful counselor-client relationships are characterized by nurturance, collaboration and insight-orientation. (p. 103)

Consequently, coursework needs to integrate reflection about counselor qualities and values including nurturance, collaboration, and insight orientation. These characteristics build both empathy and understanding of the global human condition; and will provide insights on international perspectives including cultural strengths and differences. Furthermore, counselors need opportunities to explore and define their values and personal characteristics, articulating what they need to know for practice. Whether they need knowledge of career counseling theory and practice; and on going computer and technology skills that give attention to online searches and research application skills or special internships, activities need to permit counselors to test their online comfort level in safety and with supervision by experienced online career counselors. With supervision from experienced online counselors, counselors will be able to integrate their skills and values in a safe environment as they experience how to be with and respond to clients through written texts.

VALUING COUNSELOR CHARACTERISTICS

As noted in earlier chapters, legislation in the 1980s made possible the expanded programs to meet the growing demand for career services resulting from plant closings. However, this expansion may have come with a price that ignored counselor characteristics in place of career competencies. We all know these competencies: career development theory; individual and group counseling skills; individual/group assessment; information resources; program promotion, management and implementation; coach, consultation and performance improvements; diverse populations; supervision; ethical/legal issues; research/evaluation; and technology.

Although it is important to train counselors in technology, it is equally important to provide opportunities for counselors to reflect on past traditions, meaning, the importance of counselor characteristics as the basis for successful counseling outcomes.

The Person–Technician View

For instance, Brammer and Shostrom (1968, cited in Hansen et al., 1972), as a base for their book, discussed counselor characteristics as the person–technician balance by listing five focal points:

1. The counselor is engaged in helping others but is also a human being with personal weaknesses and problems of his or her own.

2. The counselor is an expert in helping others but has no mystical or technical solutions. Technical training can be helpful but only through continuous attempts to increase self-understanding and awareness can he or she believe in what he or she is attempting to do with clients.
3. Both the client and the counselor are unique individuals.
4. Therefore, counseling must be viewed as a workshop for the growth of both individuals.
5. The central emphasis for the counselor must be the development of a core of valid techniques along with the flexibility for adding new ideas and discarding old approaches. Counseling techniques should be developed for the client and most of all, be consistent with the counselor.

The authors believed that counseling should not be guided primarily by one theory of thought, but viewed rather as "a dynamic interplay of unique relationship between two distinctive individuals" (p.177).

APA View

Earlier still, in 1947, the American Psychological Association (APA) Committee on Training in Clinical Psychology compiled the following list of 15 ideal traits for a counselor:

1. Superior intellectual ability and judgment.
2. Originality, resourcefulness, and versatility.
3. Fresh and insatiable curiosity; self-learner.
4. Interest in persons as individuals rather than as material for manipulation—a regard for the integrity of other persons.
5. Insight into own personality characteristics; sense of humor.
6. Sensitivity to the complexities of motivation.
7. Tolerance.
8. Ability to adapt "therapeutic" attitude; ability to establish warm and effective relationships with others.
9. Industry; methodological work habits; ability to tolerate pressure.
10. Acceptance of responsibility.
11. Tact and cooperativeness.
12. Integrity, self-control, and stability.
13. Discriminating sense of ethical values.

14. Breadth of cultural background—"educated man."
15. Deep interest in psychology, especially in its clinical aspect.

ACA Counselor Preparation Publication

Hansen et al. (1972) cited characteristics found in a publication by the National American Vocational Guidance Association (1949) on counselor preparation. General counselor characteristics were stated as, "a deep interest in people, and patience with them, sensitivity to the attitudes and actions of others, emotional stability and objectivity, a capacity for being trusted by others and respect of facts" (p.160). In addition, the Association for Counselor Education and Supervision (1964, cited in Hansen et al., 1972), indicated counselors needed six basic qualities:

1. Belief in each individual.
2. Commitment to individual human values.
3. Alertness to the world.
4. Open-mindedness.
5. Understanding of self.
6. Professional commitment.

EARLY THEORISTS

The characteristics just listed demonstrate what earlier theorists considered the most significant resource a counselor brings to the relationship, that is, his or her self. In other words the counselor needs to experience him or her self as a person of worth and individuality before he or she can afford such a luxury to a client. This concept is what was known as the *counselor as a technique*.

Drefyus

According to Dreyfus (1967, cited in Hansen et al., 1972), "it is not a counselor's training and what he (or she) does as a counselor, but rather his (or her) ability to be human that is of prime importance" (p. 160).

Whitaker

Whitaker (1975) advocated the importance of being with clients versus reliance on theory or technique. Theory, he noted, is useful to beginners, but counselors, he warned, need to be themselves. Pointing to Paul Tillich's (1952) concept of "being is becoming," Whitaker stated:

> Therapists that base their work on theory are likely to substitute dispassionate technology for caring ... Instead of having the courage just to "be" with families and help them grapple with their problems. (p. 279)

Whitaker suggested that counselors attend to their own behavior first, by going inside themselves to examine their own responses, anxieties, values, and beliefs. By first looking at their own assumptions and fears, counselors will begin to trust themselves and be in a better position to engage clients in looking at their issues. This is consistent with feminist therapy and multicultural approaches.

Feminist and Multicultural Perspectives

Feminist and multicultural perspectives look not to technique or theory, rather, these perspectives ask the counselor to re-examine the values and structure of our society and how, as counselors, we might be perpetuating or changing those attitudes that prove destructive for clients. In this perspective counselors learn to trust themselves in order to engage clients to look at their own values and issues.

Graduate School Experience

Since graduate school, I haven't given much thought to the concept of the *counselor as technique.* I accepted the concept, considering it a universal among counselors. I believed it was a distinguishing characteristic of a good counselor. However, as I reviewed the various codes of ethics and standards of practice as well as literature regarding the paraprofessional field of coaching, I recognized that over the years, perhaps something has been lost in terms of counselor training. It may be that in defining competencies, and in articulating standards for practice, our profession has come to favor the skill of counseling over its art. This means the concept of the counselor as technique may have been traded for counselor competencies, skills, and tangible outcome measures, versus the early measures of successful counseling as observed in a client's ability to gain insight or measured by their expression of increased life satisfaction.

Current Observations

A return to our roots, viewing career counseling as a way to develop the human potential in both the counselor and the client, is an important step in designing new programs for counselor education. It is a step in the renewal of counseling as an art versus a technology for change. The art of our profession needs to apply not just to helping clients renew their lives, it follows we need to apply our skills and insights to our own renewal and growth.

By focusing on values and integrating values into counselor training programs we not only will enhance and improve our counselor education programs, we will operate consistently with the values of the profession. Interestingly in an interview with ACA's former president, Donna Ford, published in *Counseling Today*, (1999), Ford outlined six values she has incorporated into the ACA strategic plan. These values are not that far afield from those offered by earlier leaders including, "caring for self and others, respecting diversity, encouraging positive change, acquiring and using knowledge, empowering leadership and promoting linkages."

LESSON I I: THE COUNSELOR AS THE CURRICULUM

Reflections based on practice have led me to my final lesson on the road, new counselor education programs for online career counseling practice need to be grounded in what I characterize as the *counselor as curriculum*. This lesson flows from the others, namely that if client voices inform our practice, so do counselor voices. It follows that counselor voices are equally important to the development of new curricula for adding to the growing demand for online career counseling services.

A model based on the *counselor as the curriculum* concept would allow for additional advantages, such as strategies for managing burnout.

THE COUNSELOR AS CURRICULUM ADDRESSES COUNSELOR BURNOUT

One of the concerns I regularly hear from counselors leaving the field, as well as from social workers and others in direct service roles, is *burnout*. When I ask these people what strategies they have used to arm themselves against burnout, to wrap themselves (so to speak), to nurture or provide self-care, the question is met with puzzlement. Many do not have a clue. And, when I press further asking what they learned about managing burnout in graduate school, the response is a laugh. This reaction reminds me of the practicum students I supervised over the years. Often, their supervisors appeared more interested in their attendance and paper work than whether they were integrating counseling skills for their own growth and as a strategy for serving clients.

I propose we will fail aspiring counselors unless we develop new programs incorporating renewal issues. We need to design programs that allow counselors to examine their values, nurture their creativity, and celebrate opportunities for their own self-care and growth. To be online means an opportunity for counselors to utilize their spontaneity and creativity as they respond to clients. It is an opportunity to draw upon all the counselor skills they have integrated into their lives and practice settings. To do this they must be able to use themselves as resources and call on experiences, trusting their instincts and creative responses. How else will clients learn to trust their instincts if not through the modeling and expertise offered by qualified career counselors?

SUMMARY

Interactive and qualitative research methods provide insights and new understanding for career counseling professionals to uncover best practices as counseling theories and skills are translated over the Internet. Evidence from interactive research suggests that online clients value counselor credentials as an indicator for reliable help. Credentials also serve to build trust between the client and counselor as well as protect the public interest without legislation. Furthermore, a new career counseling credential will spark the need to develop counselor programs. A value based curriculum integrating counselor characteristics and strategies for self-care will provide counselors the opportunity for renewal. By providing counselors an opportunity to be full partners in the development of new programs, we will model for them the very goals we articulate for clients, that is, the full development of their potential.

As the millennium unfolds, rather than competencies alone, counselor values and characteristics may better define for the public who is qualified to provide career counseling and who is offering something different. New counselor programs and career counseling credentials can also provide the catalyst for a paradigm shift without the need for legislation, and reflect Ford's call for: "Alignment of our values with all association activities."

DISCUSSION QUESTIONS

1. Why are qualitative research methods important to the development of the new medium of online career services?
2. Describe the client characteristics outlined in this qualitative study regarding online clients.
3. Which client characteristics and/or issues are important to your practice and why?
4. What is your assessment of the need for a new credential for online career counseling? Do you think one is needed? Why or Why not?
5. What are your views about designing a new curriculum based on a model of the counselor as the curriculum? What is the basis for your view? Be prepared to provide evidence to support your view, for or against, the counselor as the curriculum.

10

Emerging Practice Models

When you travel, you experience, in a very practical way, the act of rebirth. You confront completely new situations, the day passes more slowly, and on most journeys you don't even understand the language the people speak. So you are just like a child just out of the womb. You begin to attach much more importance to the things around you because your survival depends on them. You begin to be more accessible to others because they may be able to help you in difficult situations. And you accept any small favor from the gods with great delight, as if it were an episode you would remember for the rest of your life. At the same time, since all things are new, you see only the beauty in them, and you feel happy to be alive. That's why a religious pilgrimage has always been one of the most objective ways of achieving insight.

—Coelho (1995, p. 32)

Like Coelho's hero in *The Pilgrimage*, I found insight on my journey by attaching, "importance to the things around." I found my way by listening to client voices, those filled with hope, trust, and appreciation for this new medium. And, like a child, I may "remember for the rest of my life," their words and messages as I continue to reflect on and apply these lesson in my practice and for the development of new practice models.

REFLECTIONS ON PRACTICE

As a narrative study, my reflections on practice have limitations. First, the study is limited to the practice of e-mail career counseling sponsored by the OCC for a diverse population of adults between August

1998 and January 1999. This means the findings are specific to this population under these circumstances. The study is not intended to be comprehensive nor focused on technology issues reported in recent literature like security for online client records and the lack of regulations and laws to catch up with the explosive use of the new technology (Haas, 2000). As a narrative based on interactive methods, I have focused on the human side of career counseling technology and the voices of its users. Not all voices have been included nor all issues presented such as those writing about hostile and abusive work environments, how to handle bad performance reviews, and/or lack of recognition. I did not track demographic information except very generally. Nor did the study focus on college and university career centers although many suggestions are applicable to those catering to adults and alumni. As a narrative, the study is restricted to e-mail career counseling between one individual counselor and 850 individual clients. And, because these services are new, I may "only see the beauty in them."

ONLY THE BEAUTY

However, by restricting the study to e-mail career counseling and reflections on client voices, *seeing only the beauty*, a unique counselor–client perspective emerges providing insights for application. What makes this experience unique is not only the setting and overwhelming response from clients, it is the luxury afforded by OCC. With the opportunity to devote my time to full time practice via the Internet, I was freed to reflect on the meanings and possibilities this medium offers the future. Although I focused on only one model, OCC's confidential and free e-mail career counseling service, many other models are possible and undoubtedly will emerge. Whether new models emerge as value added or fee-for-service, development will follow in any setting offering support levels similar to those provided by OCC: financial, professional, or technical support.

In addition, I enjoyed the vicarious support of career counseling professionals from coast to coast. It came from JoAnne Harris-Bowlsbey, past president of NCDA and executive director of ACT Educational Technology Center, Hunt Valley, MD, and Shannon Anderson in San Diego where she directs the Career Counseling Extension Program at the University of California, San Diego (UCSD). In between, I found enthusiasm and encouragement from my colleagues at Options Career and Resource Center, Houston; Resource Careers,

Inc., Cleveland; Career Development Services, Rochester, New York; and colleagues at Interim Career Consulting, currently Spherion Corporation, Indianapolis. As they learned what I was doing, all were very positive and encouraging. Their support further energized and empowered my efforts to discover and share what works.

Consequently, I trust my journey along the road to online practice during my 5 months with OCC and its 11 lessons provides useful insights to the emerging body of knowledge on career counseling over the Internet. I trust, too, the study provides perspectives, which inspire new research efforts, practice models which bridge a paradigm shift within the profession.

SUGGESTIONS FOR CURRICULUM DEVELOPMENT

As a career counselor, qualitative researcher, and adult educator, I look back on my original thoughts about this book as a vehicle to share my experiences, and perhaps serve as secondary text. I planned the book in a sequential fashion, one chapter building on the other. Yet as I re-read the content and reflect on its 11 lessons, I see many chapters may stand independently. And, on further reflection believe the 11 lessons may offer a framework for curriculum development for new coursework on career counseling over the Internet or for ongoing professional development. Each lesson could serve as content for workshop topics offered individually. Topics could be offered in combination or even integrated into counselor internships.

Whether topics are offered individually or in some combination, the curriculum content should include a review of the ethical codes and standards of practice for WebCounseling and Internet career counseling, as well as competencies specific to the topics. The delivery and format of the content may vary by instructor. However, I believe new practice models require an interactive, experiential approach with an emphasis on the counselor as curriculum. This concept is similar to what Belenky, Chincy, Goldberger, and Tarule (1986) called *connected teaching*.

Connected teaching calls for an emphasis on connection and relationship (rather than separation and autonomy) with both the knowledge learned and with the facilitator and other learners. By this, Belenky et al. meant that women learn best in environments where knowledge that comes from life experiences as women, is valued and where the knowledge that is presented helps women see themselves as creators of knowledge. Like Belenky, Miller (1986) noted the importance of connectedness in training women for competence and effectiveness stating:

> The girl and woman often feel a sense of effectiveness as arising out of emotional connections and as bound up with and feeding back into them. This is very different from a sense of effectiveness (or power) based in lone action and in acting against or over others. (p. 16)

If you substitute the word counselor/s for "girl, woman and women" and life experience as a counselor/s for "life experiences as women," you will have a close description of the "counselor as curriculum." This concept values counselor knowledge and his or her experience base. It invites counselors to become co-creator in new curriculum to meet their needs. By affording counselors opportunities as co-creators of curriculum, new strategies for counselor renewal and commitment to the field should follow, as well as enthusiasm for online practice. In this way, too, counselors may view technology as a tool to reach underserved clients rather than a replacement of themselves.

11 LESSONS FROM THE ROAD

A brief summary on the 11 lessons follows incorporating how each may be the subject of course content for an emerging practice model.

Lesson 1: Valuing Written Texts

Whenever I hear a counselor downplay online counseling, emphasizing that counseling cannot take place without the visual and nonverbal exchange that happens in a face-to-face situation, I immediately think of my early reactions to this medium. It took receiving and reading literally thousands of e-mails from clients, sharing intimate details of their lives, for me to know and experience the power and value of written texts. Not only did I discover nonverbal clues within their written messages, I learned to translate and apply individual counseling skills as I responded to their clues. I learned, too, that just as we clarify with clients in person something that is said or communicated nonverbally, we can do this in written texts. Client voices in written texts speak their own language, whether they share an experience, outcome, or send a thank you note, these messages teach us that the client counselor relationship rather than being compromised online can be both established and maintained via written texts. And, as Lee (1998) reminded us:

We have an emerging generation for whom interaction via the computer is common, natural, and fully accepted means of communication. This generation of potential clients is used to less actual personal contact and greater interaction in cyberspace in many aspects of their lives. To think that clients in the new century would not expect to access Internet counseling services is probably foolish and shortsighted on our part.

From a curriculum standpoint, a workshop on written texts provides an opportunity for counselors to learn guidelines for applying counseling skills online. By taking an interactive approach to the topic, counselors can review and renew their skills by sharing past experiences and comparing how their experiences match or do not match examples in the book. By also reviewing ethical codes and standards for practice, counselors will learn how to integrate and apply their skills online in an ethical and effective manner. The review may serve equally to acknowledge individual counselor strengths, affirming each in the process. Furthermore, the curriculum will include attention to each counselor's own philosophy of career counseling providing guidance for participants to articulate and write their own definitions and goals of the online career counseling process.

Lesson 2: Understanding the Power of Anonymity

The power of anonymity afforded by the Internet is an important topic for counselors to understand. Just as Rogers (1942) introduced the power of unconditional positive regard and empathy in the client–counselor relationship, departing from the straightforward trait-and-factor approach of Parsons (1909), I believe the Internet holds another departure and new power—the power of anonymity. By providing clients with the opportunity to ask questions, anonymously, an unexpected confidentiality follows, allowing clients who, out of shame, fear, or embarrassment, might otherwise not step forward to do so. With the opportunity to ask questions anonymously and confidentially, a new type of access makes career services available to underserved clients.

Consequently, the very concerns many counselors express about the Internet creating barriers to the development of the client–counselor relationship may not necessarily be true. By examining client messages, counselors can view and judge for themselves the value and power of anonymity in serving an online population. Like in-person clients, counselors will learn strategies for informing and assuring clients about confidentially and/or its risks over the Internet, allowing clients the choice to utilize or not, services in this medium. Again, this part of the curriculum will allow for a review of ethical issues and practice sessions for online application.

Lesson 3: Viewing Career Counseling as Personal Counseling

Like Lesson 2, Lesson 3 speaks to the personal nature of career counseling over the Internet and how to safeguard the client–counselor relationship. I believe safeguarding the relationship online is the same as safeguarding the relationship in person. We do this by being good professionals and following best practices. Also, we pay attention to our clients and respect their needs and risk factors. This is evident in a review of client questions. Rarely does a client write asking a strictly informational question like, "What is the difference between a chronological and functional resume?" Instead, they ask about the best resume for their circumstances, adding in great detail individual differences that are often related to gender, class, ethnic background, and/or cultural differences, with many touching on discrimination issues. This is just one of the reasons I believe that qualified career counselors rather than paraprofessionals are needed, even when career services are restricted to job search practices. Career counseling is personal counseling, not a mechanical skill practiced by anyone. Course content on this topic would naturally focus on individual counseling skills and how to translate these online in an effective and ethical manner. The course content would also address ethical dilemmas and the Practitioner's Guide to Ethical Decision-Making. Using an experiential focus would allow counselors to present actual situations they have faced for case review and analysis.

Lesson 4: Listening to Client Voices

Listening to client voices is one of the most important lessons along my road, which could be an umbrella topic for a semester's curriculum. Clients have much to teach us, particularly their views on confidentiality, anonymity, and access. It is their voices that first prompted me to explore online services. Their written message confirmed that the medium was reaching a global population of underserved clients in the United States and more than a dozen countries (Burma, Austria, Canada, China, Ghana, Holland, India, Italy, Mexico, Nigeria, Pakistan, Russia, Switzerland, Thailand, Sweden, Venezuela, and the United

Kingdom). By focusing the curriculum on client voices, particular attention will be paid to (a) the characteristics of clients, (b) typical questions asked, and (c) dealing with personal data. Like valuing written texts, the focus of this workshop will (a) examine written messages for clues about personal data or affective phrases like, "feeling more relaxed," "giving me insight," "finding specific answers," "giving me peace of mind," "gaining a grip," and "time to find someone who can be supportive!"; (b) observe client movement or behavioral signs of resolution, such as language indicating a readiness for change, and/or congruence between the client's language and actions they describe; (c) choose a format or turnaround time for responses to clients as well as whether the service will be offered free or for a fee; and (d) review ethical concerns, including a broader understanding about privacy issues as specified in our profession by three codes of professional ethics. The curriculum would also give attention to counselors' voices, allowing them to express and write their views or philosophy of practice for online career counseling over the Internet.

Lesson 5: Bridging Cultural Difference

This lesson could spin off several workshops or the expansion of academic courses focusing on immigration issues, destination services, and effective skills for dealing with cultural issues and differences. For example Sue and Sue (1990) recommended influencing skills versus affective skills, noting, "to avoid placing Asian Americans in the uncomfortable and oppressed position," counselors should utilize influencing versus attending skills, that is, they should provide clients with the advice and information they seek rather than relying on reflection of feelings. Sue and Sue (1990) noted a study by Atkinson et al. (1978), in which the findings showed that "counselors who use the directive approach were rated more credible and approachable than those using the nondirective counseling approach" (p. 69). Examining and discussing these studies is one way to bridge cultural differences.

Internet career counseling offers a fresher approach, allowing counselors to examine written text freed from biases that typically are experienced during in-person sessions. Building on this concept, it would be equally important to draw on the resources of counselors in attendance, allowing them to be co-creators in the curriculum, defining for the group what is important to integrate regarding cultural differences and strengths. Part of building bridges occurs through networking, a critical skill to teach international clients, particularly those wanting to immigrate to the United States. It is also a critical skill for counselors to know and apply in their daily lives. If counselors do not network for themselves, it may be difficult for them to see or teach the skill's value for new immigrants. Networking could be part of the curriculum on cultural differences or could stand alone as a separate workshop.

Lesson 6: Setting Online Boundaries

Louann Kummerer, senior consultant for Interim Career Consulting, the outplacement branch of Interim Career Services, currently Spherion Corporation, shareed the list of dos and don'ts she developed for working with career coaches online. This list bears repeating and could serve as a guide to help counselors develop their own list of boundaries regarding:

   A. Legal Policy: Three key points:
      1. Career coaching services are provided only to adults over 18 years of age.
      2. Career coaches must refrain from providing legal advice to those contacting us.
      3. Career coaches must provide options; not advice!
   B. Style: use a standard greeting and closing, such as:
      1. Greeting: "Greetings"; "Hello"; or the person's name.
      2. Closing: "Thank you for your question and best of success in your future career endeavor."
      3. Signing: "Career Coach."
   C. Content: Whenever providing options, use a disclaimer statement.

A workshop focused on boundary issues and disclaimer statements provides an opportunity for counselors to again review ethical codes and standards of practice over the Internet. It also provides an opportunity to work together collaboratively suggesting, designing, and developing new policies and disclaimer statements appropriate for career counseling practice. By taking an experiential approach, participants can help guide the content of this session based on a combination of factors from their own practice, including counselors who may have online experience already.

In addition, content should engage counselors in understanding the larger picture that consulting skills play in online practice. Savickas (1996) noted the importance of influencing public policy stating:

Counselors can contribute important perspectives and ideas to the national dialogue about public policy concerning (a) goals for career intervention, (b) who will plan and who will deliver career interventions, and (c) to whom and how career intervention will be made accessible. (p. 4)

Lesson 7: Affirming Clients Through Assessments

Clients say they feel affirmed by their test results. Affirmation appears to take place when the results of testing or an assessment session brings to light a client's strengths, new insights about preferences, and/or confirmation about new directions to pursue. Rarely does the client deny the tangible results from the testing, particularly, those articulating the client's potential. Having something tangible in black and white, so to speak, confirms an inner hunch or sparks an old dream. Results like these can be very energizing for clients. Testing provides hope as well as a starting point.

Because counselors know a great deal about providing assessments for clients, this topic may require only brief review. Instead, the focus could center on practicing or translating assessment skills online. Again, taking an experiential approach allows counselors to shape the curriculum and, rather than focusing on the content of assessment selection, counselors may prefer a self-assessment process for their own growth. Utilizing self-assessments exercises may allow counselors to experience the affirmation clients feel when accurate and appropriate assessment instruments are available to them. It would also give counselors an opportunity for self-renewal and provide strategies for their own career management and self-care.

Just as Seligman (1980) recommended testing as an integral part of the counseling relationship, it can provide counselors in professional development sessions similar opportunities for their own growth by the following actions:

- Promoting more relevant and focused discussion.
- Stimulating and guide exploration and information seeking.
- Indicating the likelihood that certain events will happen.
- Clarifying self-concept.
- Promoting translations of interests, abilities, and personality dimensions into occupational terms.
- Suggesting options or alternatives.
- Facilitating the ordering or ranking of options.

Assessment or what lay people call career testing has great appeal to both clients and counselors alike. For counselors, it can be a concrete and valuable tool to analyze or determine issues or categorize client difficulties. Furthermore, it can provide the most appropriate referrals and links to additional resources. Knowing how to and encouraging counselors to use assessment tools for their own career development and self-care is equally important.

Lesson 8: Providing Online Information and Referral

If there is any argument demonstrating that online services extend access and a unique service for what professionals call special populations, it is illustrated by the fourth competency for certified career counselors, Information Resources and Referral. Clients reluctant to step forward out of embarrassment or for any reason, may not only find greater access to career counselors online, they may find almost instant answers through appropriate links and resources at their fingertips. To become familiar with the vast array of resources and to understand which are the most appropriate for which individual or special population is a skill in itself, particularly, in an age of specialization. Clients are often confused about how to work through the maze of information that is available. This competency is all the more critical when someone's circumstances represent more than one special population. That is why I contend that working online requires experienced counselors with a strong knowledge base and an understanding of special populations. A workshop or program on this topic would focus on special populations, reviewing sensitive issues and cultural differences related to each population. It would also include how to search online and locate resources, identifying those in the local, national and global community for reference.

Lesson 9: Embracing Technology

Lesson 9, embracing technology, looked at the human face of online services rather than technology issues per se, such as security, handling online client records, and the lack of regulations and laws to catch up with the explosive use of the new technology (Haas, 2000). Because there is available literature on technology topics, I left this discussion to others in an attempt to address motivational issues for embracing technology. By this I mean, yes, there are problems and barriers with technology. And, yes, counselors need to keep up with technology and learn all they can about implementing new technologies. However, if there is no support for what counselors are trying to do (new courses), new technology will not necessarily be the answer.

To embrace technology requires resources and support. With the right resources and support counselors will take time to learn the latest in technology, keep up with the changes in ethical standards for online practice, and embrace technology willingly. Whether a counselor is in the business community, government setting, private practice or the academic world, support can and will enable them to make the transition without legislation. Without support, they are likely to hit stonewalls and label technology a barrier instead of tool for the advancement of client transformation. I suggest curriculum for this topic focus on three areas. First is the examination of policy issues related to technology such as use policies, disclaimer statements, and the boundaries of online practice. Second, is the exploration of counselor attitudes and fears about technology and online career counseling. Group discussions coupled with the examination of client voices in written texts can uncover or identify counselors' real and perceived barriers in utilizing the medium. Identifying barriers would also include motivational issues as well as strategies to garner the support and resources for overcoming barriers. The third area would address action plans for embracing technology. Written technology plans, whether in individual or group format should outline specific goals and objectives for action steps to overcome barriers and embrace technology.

Lesson 10: Developing New Credentials

With the retirement of the NBCC National Certified Career Counselor specialty, the practice of online career counseling has no way to distinguish itself and is often confused with career coaching. As a specialty of WebCounseling, a new credential for career counselors would give clients a reliable way to distinguish who is qualified to provide career counseling online and who is offering something different, such as coaching or advising.

Our ethical codes, standards for practice and career counseling competencies, provide the framework for coursework related to skill development for this specialty. However, as we move forward to design new programs, it is important that we not emphasize skill over art of counseling, lest we forget the main ingredient for successful career counseling outcomes, that is, the counselor–client relationship. As Stoltz-Loike (1996) said:

> The counselor's respect for the client's perspective dramatically affects the success of counseling sessions ... successful counselor-client relationships are characterized by nurturance, collaboration and insight-orientation. (p. 103)

Consequently, all coursework aimed at a new credentials needs to integrate reflections on counselor qualities and values, including nurturance, collaboration, and insight orientation, all characteristics that develop empathy and understanding of the global human condition. Counselor supervision and internships need to integrate attention to and self-care for counselors. Without attention to self-care, we will see an exodus from the field as counselors suffer burnout or grow tired from greater demands placed on them. More than anything else, new curriculums need to provide opportunities for counselors to validate their experience, feel a sense of renewal, and find respect for and draw on the creative spirit within. Counselors need to trust and value themselves. By knowing themselves and identifying their values, counselors will gain a deeper sense of who they are as persons. Without this, they won't be in a position to guide a global clientele. Coursework for a new credential needs to recognize opportunities for counselors to integrate their counseling skills and values in their daily lives so that their online practice becomes an extension of what they do in person, not different from or something separate.

Lesson 11: Recognizing the Counselor as Curriculum

Coursework for new credentials will develop and flow from an approach based on the *counselor as curriculum*. This concept is consistent with feminist and multicultural perspectives, which look not to technique or theory, but rather ask the counselor to re-examine the values and structure of our society and how, as counselors, we might perpetuate or change those attitudes that prove destructive for clients. In this way counselors begin to trust them selves, and trust clients to engage in looking at their own values and behaviors. In workshops, this means emphasizing the importance of counselor values and characteristics as the basis for successful counseling outcomes. For example, in 1964 the Association for Counselor Education and Supervision indicated that the counselor should have six basic qualities:

1. Belief in each individual.
2. Commitment to individual human values.
3. Alertness to the world.
4. Open-mindedness.
5. Understanding of self.
6. Professional commitment.

These characteristics demonstrate what earlier theorists considered the most significant resource a counselor brings to the relationship, that is, his or her self. Using interactive exercises involving autobiographies, journals, and genograms, counselors will have the opportunity for reflection to identify their values and characteristics, thus experiencing a sense of renewal, worth and individuality.

Interestingly, the six counselor characteristics outlined decades ago, are not far afield from those emphasized by ACA's past president, Donna Ford. In an interview, Ford outlined six values she has incorporated into the ACA strategic plan. These are: "caring for self and others, respecting diversity, encouraging positive change, acquiring and using knowledge, empowering leadership and promoting linkages" (Ford, 1999).

TOMORROW'S PRACTICE MODELS

I am aware that critics may judge the value I place on listening to clients as inconclusive, not based on hard research. These critics may discount qualitative methods as too subjective, finding the narrative without merit. However, I believe the narrative worthy and consistent with new traditions in our field (Paisely, 1997). Older traditions, too, recognized the importance of interactive and qualitative methods to inform theory. Rogers (1974) looked to his clients to inform his theory. Furthermore, he attributed his own growth to his profound respect for the client–counselor relationship, writing: "If I subtract from my work the learnings I have gained from deep relationships with my clients and group participants, I would be nothing" (p. 120).

It is hard to believe that Frank Parson's early inspirations for the establishment of the Vocational Guidance Bureau was not the result of listening to the young adults and immigrants he served. These traditions greatly influence my recommendations and/or lessons from the road.

Listening to client and counselor voices provides a fresh approach to online practice and positive change. As the millennium unfolds, rather than competencies alone, counselor characteristics may prove the catalyst for creating and implementing new practice models as well as a paradigm shift, one not requiring legislation to protect public interest as we implement career counseling over the Internet.

SUMMARY

Counselor and client voices are emerging and telling us to press forward with career counseling over the Internet. I trust this study offers a groundbreaking look at what many online clients have to tell us. Although their voices are expressed to only one counselor, it is my hope their messages resonate with others and spark more interest in research, particularly with an emphasis on client and counselor voices. Client voices (the users of online career counseling) are an important guide to help professionals examine and develop appropriate programs and strategies for implementation over the Internet. Attention to client voices will also serve for the improvement of practice models if we but listen with our hearts and minds. Furthermore, utilizing experimental and interactive methods, the *counselor as curriculum*, may hold the secret of renewing and reinventing counselors as well as their instructors. For as Paulo discovers at the end of *The Pilgrimage*, his mysterious guide, Petrus, believes:

> You can learn only through teaching. We have been together here on the road to Santiago, but while you were learning the practices, I learned the meaning of them. By taking on the role of guide, I was able to find my own true path. (Coelho, 1995, pp. 191–192)

DISCUSSION QUESTIONS

1. Which are the most important of the 11 lessons to you and why?
2. Are there other lessons you would add? Why or why not?
3. What do you believe is necessary for counselor renewal and growth?
4. Explain what Petrus means by learning happens "only through teaching." Do you agree or disagree with his view?

Appendix A: Websites

About Work	http://www.aboutwork.com
Advanced Consulting Group	http://www.advgroup.com
Alumni Net	http://www.alumnet.com
Amazon.com	http://www.amazon.com
American Corporate Counsel Association	http://www.acca.com
American Counseling Association	http://www.aca.com
American Embassies (Norwegian)	http://www.usembassy.no
American Embassies and Consulates Worldwide	http://travel.state.gov/links.html
American Federation of TV & Radio Artists	http://www.aftrasf.org
American's Job Bank	http://www.ajb.dni.us
American Immigration Lawyers Association	http://www.aila.org
American Management Association	http://www.amanet.org
American Occupational Therapy Association	http://www.aota.org
Association of Teachers of Technical Writing	http://english.ttu.edu/attw
Associations	http://www.vcanet.org/
Black Collegian	http://www.black-collegian.com/jobs
Books online/Southwestern publishing	http://www.swep.com
California Civil Service	http://www.spb.ca.gov
Career Action Center	http://www.careeraction.org
Career Development Services	http://www.careerdev.org
Career Karma Magazine	http://www.careerkarma.com
Career Magazine	http://www.careermag.com
Career Mosaic	http://www.careermosaic.com
Career Zone.com	http://www.careerzone.com
Career Path	http://www.careerpath.com
Caribbean Resourcing Solutions, LTD	http://www.caribinfo.com/jobs/default.htm
Center for Career/Life Planning	http://admin.cpp-db.com/C/cclpin
Chronicle of Higher Education	http://chronicle.com/jobs/
Chronicle of Philanthropy	http://www.philanthropy.com
Colleges and Universities	http://www.mit.edu:8001/people/ cdemello/V.html
Community Colleges	http://www.utexas.edu/world/univ/
Department of Veteran Affairs	http://www.va.gov/jobs/monthly.htm
Dictionary of Occupational Titles/O*Net	http://wwwdoleta.gov/programs/onet/
Directory of Executive Recruiters	http://www.kennedyinfo.com/hr/hrcder.htm
Directory of Executive Recruiters	1-603-585-6544

Embassies	http://www.embassy.org/embassies/
Event Planning Groups	http://eventsource.com/cf/resources/
Excite Careers Network	http://www.excite.com/careers
Federal Government Agencies	http://fedworld.gov
Federal Government Agencies	http://usgovinfo.miningco.com/blemploy.htm
Feminist Majority on Breast Cancer	http://www.feminist.org/other/bs/ bchome.html
Financial Aid	http://www.finaid.org
Financial Planners	http://www.icfp.org
Find Law	http://www.findlaw.com
Food Service Industry	http://hrpublications.hypermart.net/food-retail.htm
Foundation Center	http://www.fdncenter.org
Gay Workplace Issues Homepage	http://www.nyu.edu/pages/sls/gaywork
Getting Started in Technical Communications	http://www.ace1.com/webbook.htm
Healthcare Online	http://www.healthcareers.com/Jonllie.htm
Home Business	http://www.usahomebusiness.com/book.htm
Home Office Association	http://www.hoaa.com
Home-Based Working Moms	http://www.hbwm.com
Homeworkers.org	http://www.homeworkers.org
IBM Online Business	http://www.ibm.com/e-business
Indianapolis Public Library	http://www.imcpl.lic.in.us
Immigration Forum	http://www.immigrationformus.org
International Coach Federation	http://www/coachfederation.org
International Home Workers Association	http://www.tjobs.com
International Resources	http://internatioanl.monster.com/ workintheus
International Telework Association & Council	http://www.telelcommute.org
Job Accommodation Network	http://janweb.icdi.wvu.edu.english/contact/ htm
Job Accommodation Network	1-800-526-7234 or 1-800-526-4698
Jobs in Geology	http://alserv.rug.ac.be~gbaret/jopsearch.html
Kennedy's Pocket Guide to Deal with Recruiters	http://kennedyinfo.com/js/pocket.html
Korn/Ferry International Recruiters	http://www.kornferry.com
Library, Indianapolis	http://www.imcpl.lib.in.us
MBA	http://www.biz.colostate.edu/mba/distance/ distance/htm
Medical Associations	http://library.tmc.edu/medassoc.html
Military Transition	http://content.monster.com/military/
Monster Board	http://www.monster.com
National Association of Colleges & Employers	http://www.jobweb.org/map.htm
National Association of Public Interest Law	http://www.napal.org/links
National Association of Asian American Professionals	http://www.naaap.org
National Association of Social Workers	http://www.nasw.org
National Association of Certified Counselors	http://www.nbcc.org
National Organization of Gay and Lesbian Scientists	http://www.noglstlp.org
National Service	http://www.nationalservice.org
National Association of Professional Engineer	hrrp://www.nspe.org
National University	http://www.nu.edu/index/html
New Ways to Work	http://www.nww.org
New York University Career Services	http://www.nyu.edu/careerservices
Nonprofit Center with Searchable Databases	http://www.opporunitynocs.org/home
Nonprofit/Action Without Boarders	http://www.idealist.org
Occupational Outlook Handbook	http://stats.bls.gov/oco/oco1000.htm
Older Workers	http://www.srempoly.org
Older Workers	http://greenthumb.org/experwks.htm

One Stop Centers	http://www.ttrc.doleta.gov/onestop
Online Career Center	http://www.occ.com
Options Resource and Career Center	http://www.optionshouston.com
Personalities/Career Inventories	http://content.monster.com/tool/
	personality/links.html
Peterson's Guide	http://www.petersons.com
PGA	http://www.pga.com
Philanthropy Online	http://www.jobs.pj.org
Public Relations Society of American	http://www.prsa.org
Rainbow Book	http://www.irni.org/links.html
Recording for the Blind and Dyslexic	http://www.rfbd.org
Resource Careers	http://www.resourcecareers.com
San Diego School Districts	http://www.sdcoe.k12.ca.us/hr/distemp.html
Science of Soil Journal	http://www.hintze.online.com/sos
Showbiz Jobs	http://www.showbizjobs.com
Single Mothers Newsletter/Job Listings	http://execpc.com/~philsch/newspaper.html
Skills2000	http://www.microsoft.com/skills2000/intern
Small Business Administration	http://www.sbaonlin.sba.gov
Small Office Computing Magazine	http://www.smalloffice.com
Society for Human Resource Management	http://www.shrm.or/hrlinks/
Society for Technical Communications	http://www.stc-va.org
Sports Industry	http://www.onlinesports.com
States (California example)	http://www.state.ca.us
Student Financial Aid	http://www.ed.gov/prog_info/SFA/Student
	Guide
Tech Center FSU	http://www.aus.fsu.edu/techcntr
Thomas E. Bliss& Associates	http://www.etbliss.com
Time Warner Telecom, Inc.	http://www.prnewswire.com
UCLA Online Learning	http://www.onlinelearning.net
United Way, Indianapolis	http://www.uwci.org/links.html
United Way, National Directory	http://dir.unitedway.org/
University Career Centers	http://www.jobweb.org/catapult/
	homepage.htm
US School Districts	http://www.jobweb.org/searchschools/
Vocational Rehabilitation by State	http://trfn.clpgh.org/srac/state-vr.html
Volunteers	http://www.servenet.org/
Wall Street Journal	http://www.careers.wsj.com
Wellness Councils of America	http://www.welcoa.org/
Womeswire (best companies)	http://www.womenswire.com/work/work.html
Work at Home Mom's Magazine	http://www.wahm.com
Working Woman Magazine	http://www.workingwoman.com
Yahoo Classified	http://.yahoo.com/employment.html

Appendix B: Databases

Career Counseling

Center for Career/Life Planning   http://admin.cpp-db.com/C/cclpin
One stop Career Centers   http://www.ttrc.doleta.gov/onestop
National Career Development Association   http://www.ncda.org
National Board for Certified Counselors   http://www.nbcc.org
University Career Centers   http://www.jobweb.org/catapult/
    homepage.htm

Education and Training

Alumni Net   http://www.alumnet.com
College Net   http://www.collegenet.com
Colleges and Universities   http://www.utexas.edu/world/univ
Find Aid   http://www.finaid.org
Financial Aid US News and World Report   http://www.usnews.com/usnews/edu/
    dollars/ff_web.htm
Peterson's Education Center   http://www.petersons.com

Internships

Bureau of Apprenticeship and Training   http://www.doleta.gov/individ/apprent.htm
College and University Career Centers   http://www.jobweb.org/cata-
    pult/homepage.htm
Corporation for National Service   http://www.nationalservice.org
Internship Programs   http://www.internshipprograms.com/
Microsoft Skills2000 Program   http://www.microsoft.com/skills2000

Job Postings

America's Job Bank   http://www.ajb.dni.us
Career Mosaic   http://www.careermosaic.com
Career Path   http://www.careerpath.com
Forbes List of Best 200 Small Companies   http://www.forbes.com/tool/toolbox/
    200best
Monster.com   http://www.monster.com
Nation Jobs Online Job Databases   http://www.nationjob.com

Military

Military Career Guide Online	http://www.militarycareers.com
The Officer Placement Service	http://www.troa.org/tops/
US Air Force	http://www.airforce.com
US Army	http://www.army.mil
US Coast Guard	http://www.uscg.mil/jobs
US Navy	http://www.navyjobs.com
Veterans	http://www.va.gov/jobs/monthly/htm

Occupations

America's Career Info Net	http://www.acinet.org
Careers Online Virtual Careers Show	http://www.careersonline.com/au/show/menu.html
Find Your Career: US News	http://www.usnews.com
Occupational Outlook Handbook	http://www.bls.gov:80/occhome.htm
O*Net (Dictionary of Occupational Titles, DOT)	http://www.doleta.gov/programs/onet/
Princeton Review Career Find-O'Rama	http://www.review.com/career/find/index.htm

References

Adams, S. C. (1998, June). Concerns about counseling online. Letters to the editor. *CTOnline, Special Report.* [http:www.counseling.org/ctonline/ sr598/letter1_698.htm].

American Library Association. (1948, 1961, 1980, & 1996). *Library Bill of Rights.* [http://www.ala.org/work/freedom/lbr.html].

American Counseling Association. (1994). *ACA Code of ethics and standards of practice.* Alexandria, VA: Author. [http://www.counseling.org/resources/codeofethics.htm].

American Counseling Association. (1999). *Special message: Ethical standards for internet on-line counseling.* Alexandria, VA: Author. [http://www.counseling.org/gc/cybertx.htm].

Armour, S. (1999, November 23). The new interview etiquette. *USA TODAY,* Money Section, Cover Story.

Belenky, M. F., Chincy, B. M., Goldberger, R. N., & Tarule, J. M. (1986). *Women's ways of knowing.* New York: Basic Books.

Bloom, J. W. (1997, November). NBCC WebCounseling standards. *CTOnline, Special Report.* [http://www.counseling.org/ctonline/sr598/nbcc_standards.htm].

Business Wire. (1999, December 22). *Monster.com announces record growth in 1999; Monster.com is the #1 online careers resource, according to recent November findings.* Maynard, MA: Business Wire.

Campbell, D. S. (1999, October 20). Coaches also help put skills to work on job, in life. *The Orlando Sentinel archive.* [http://archive.orlandosentinel.com @H385f096.../get_doc.pl?DBLIST =OS00&DOCNUM=6878]. 1–4

Buhrke, R. A. (1989). Incorporating lesbian and gay issues into counselor training: A resource guide. *The Journal of Counseling & Development, 68*(1), 77–80.

Coelho, P. (1995). *The pilgrimage: A contemporary quest for ancient wisdom.* San Francisco, CA: HarperSanFrancisco.

Crites, J. O. (1981). *Career counseling: Models, methods, and materials.* New York: McGraw-Hill.

Crose, R. (1990). *The three C's in counseling: Caring, challenge and commitment.* Unpublished manuscript, Ball State University at Muncie, IN.

Dewey, J. (1916). *The school and society.* Chicago, IL: The University of Chicago Press.

Dikel, M. R. (1999). *The Riley guide: Employment opportunities and job resources on the internet.* [www.rileyguide.com]

Dixon, P. (1998). *Job searching online for dummies.* Foster City, CA: IDG Books Worldwide.

Ford, D. (1999). Formatting our future: Our responsibility the potential. *Counseling Today, 5.*

Forester-Miller, H., & Davis, T. (1996). A practitioner's guide to ethical decision making. *American Counseling Association.* [http://www.counseling.org/resources/pracguide.htm.] 1–5

Guerra P. (1998, September). Career development profession debates electronic career information delivery. *Counseling Today, 1, 20, 22.*

Guerriero, J. M., & Allen, R. G. (1998). *Key questions in career counseling: Techniques to deliver effective career counseling services.* Hillsdale, NJ: Lawrence Erlbaum Associates.

Haas, C. (2000, January). Entangled in the 'net. *Counseling Today,* 26-27.

Hansen, J. C., Stevic, R. R., & Warner, R. W., Jr. (1972). *Counseling: Theory and process.* Boston, MA: Allyn & Bacon.

Harris-Bowlsbey, J. (1996). Synthesis and antithesis: Perspectives from Herr, Bloch, and Watts. *The Career Development Quarterly, 45*(1), 54–57.

Harris-Bowlsbey, J., Riley Dikel, M., & Sampson, J. P., Jr. (1998). *The Internet: A tool for career planning.* (1st ed.). Columbus, OH: National Career Development Association.

Lancy, D. F. (1993). *Qualitative research in education.* New York & London: Longman.

Lee, C. (1998, April). Counseling the challenges of cyberspace. *CTOnline, Special Report.* [http://www.counseling.org/ctonline/sr598/lee498.html197.htm].

Merriam, S. B., & Simpson, E. L. (1989). *A guide to research for educators and trainers of adults.* Malabar, FL: Krieger.

Miller, J. B. (1986). *Toward a new psychology of women.* Boston, MA: Beacon Press.

Minchin, S. (1974). *Families and family therapy.* Cambridge, MA: Harvard University Press.

Morrissey, M. (1997, November). NBCC WebCounselinbg Standards unleash intense debate. *CTOnline, Special Report.* http://www.counseling.org/ctonline/sr598/webcounseling 1197.htm.]

National Board for Certified Counselors. (1997). *NBCC Code of ethics.* Greensboro, NC: Author. [http://www.nbcc.org/ethics/nbcc-code.htm].

National Board for Certified Counselors. (1997, 1999). *Standards for ethical practice of WebCounseling*. Greensboro, NC: Author. [http://www.nbcc. org/ethics/wcstandards.htm].

National Career Development Association. (1997). *NCDA's career counseling competencies, revised version, 1997*. Columbus, OH: Author. [http://www.ncda.org/polcar.html].

National Career Development Association. (1994). *NCDA's consumer guidelines for selecting a career counselor*. Columbus, OH: Author. [http://www.ncda.org/polcons.html].

National Career Development Association. (1997). *NCDA's guidelines for the use of the Internet for provision of career information and planning services*. Columbus, OH: Author. [http://www.ncda.org/polweb.html].

Niles, S. G. (1997). Annual review: Practice and research in career counseling and development, 1996. *The Career Development Quarterly, 46*(2), 115–141.

Paisely, P. O. (1997). Personalizing our history: Profiles of theorists, researchers, practitioners, and issues. *Journal of Counseling & Development, 76*(1), 4–5.

Parsons, F. (1909). *Choosing a vocation*. Boston: Houghton Mifflin.

Rayman, J. R. (1999). Career services imperatives for the next millennium. *The Career Development Quarterly, 48*(2), 175–184.

Rogers, C. R. (1942). Counseling and psychotheraphy. Boston: Houghton Mifflin.

Rogers, C. R. (1951). *Client-centered therapy*. Boston: Houghton Mifflin.

Rogers, C. R. (1961). *On becoming a person: A therapist view of psychotherapy*. Boston: Houghton Mifflin.

Rogers, C. R. (1974). In retrospect: Forty-six years. *American Psychologist, 29*(2), 115–129.

Ruiz, N. J., & Lipford-Sanders, J. (1999, October). Online counseling: Further considerations. *Counseling Today*, 12–33.

Satir, V. (1972). *Peoplemaking*. Palo Alto, CA: Science and Behavior.

Savickas, M. L. (1996). Public policy and career counseling for the twenty-first century. *The Career Development Quarterly, 45*(1) 3–4.

Schmid, R. E. (1999, September 17). U.S. immigrant population is rising. *Seattle Times Company*. [http://seattletimes.nwsource.com/news/nation-world/htm l98/ altimmi _19990917.html]. 1

Seligman, L. (1980). *Assessment in the developmental career counseling*. Cranston, RI: Carroll Press.

Sharf, R. (1992). *Applying career development theory to counseling*. Pacific Grove, CA: Brooks/Cole.

Sirch-Stasko, M. (1998, June). No return [Letter to the editor]. *CTOnline, Special Report*. [http:www.counseling.org/ctonline/sr598/letter2_698.htm].

Stoltz-Loike, M. (1996). Annual review: Practice and research in career development and counseling. *The Career Development Quarterly, 45*(2), 99–140.

Sue, D. W., & Sue, D. (1990). *Counseling the culturally different, theory and practice.* Chichester, NY: Wiley.

Sussman, R. J. (1998, June). Counseling online. *CTOnline, Special Report.* [http://www.counseling.org/ctonline/sr598/sussman.htm].

Tillich, P. (1952). *The courage to be.* New Haven, CT & London: Yale University Press.

Tiedeman, D. V., & Miller-Tiedeman, A. L. (1988, 1989). Individual perspectives on career decision making. In R. S. Sharf (Ed). *Applying career development theory to counseling.* Pacific Grove, CA: Brooks/Cole.

United States Department of Education, National Center for Education Statistics. (1997). *Enrollment in higher education: Fall 1995* (Integrated Postsecondary Education Data Systems [IPEDS] surveys). Washington, DC: Author.

United State Department of State. *Tips for U.S. Visas: Employment-based visas.* [http://travel.state.gov/visa;employ-based.html]. Washington, DC: Author.

United State Department of State. *Tips for U.S. Visas: Immigrants.* [http://travel.state.gov/visa;immigrants.html]. Washington, DC: Author.

Watts, A. G. (1996). Toward a policy of lifelong career development: A transatlantic perspective. *The Career Development Quarterly, 45*(1), 41–53.

Watts, A. G. (1998, July). *A new concept of career for a new millennium: Implications for theory, policy and practice.* Keynote paper presented at the NCDA Seventh Global Conference, re-shaping career development in the 21st century, Chicago, IL.

Weddle, P. D. (1998, November 15–21). The best web sites for job hunters. *National Business Employment Weekly, xxx.*

Whitaker, C. A. (1975) in *Family therapy concepts and methods* (2nd ed.). Boston: Allyn & Bacon.

Witt, M. A. (1992). *Job strategies for people with disabilities: Enable yourself for today's job market.* Princeton, NJ: Peterson's Guide.

Wolf, C. J. (1994). *Developing a school or district "Acceptable use policy" for student and staff access to the internet.* Bremerton, WA: Olympic Educational Service District 114. [http://www.iupui.edu~jhuber/w220/w220d/aup.tx].

Worell J., & Remer, P. (1992). *Feminist perspectives in therapy: An empowerment model for women.* Chichester, UK: John Wiley & Sons.

Young, R. A., & Chen, C. P. (1999). Annual review: Practice and research in career counseling and development–1998. *The Career Development Quarterly, 48*(2), 98–141.

Zunker, V. G. (1994). *Career counseling, Applied concepts of life planning.* Pacific Grove, CA: Brooks/Cole.

Author Index

Subject Index